Newbery and Caldecott Awards:
A Subject Index

Denise Goetting ❧ *Susan Marshall Richard*

Sheryl Moore Curry ❧ *Betsy Bryan Miguez*

Your Trusted
Library-to-Classroom Connection.
Books, Magazines, and Online

Library of Congress Cataloging-in-Publication Data

Newbery and Caldecott awards : a subject index / Denise Goetting ... [etal.].p. cm.
Includes indexes.
  ISBN 1-58683-083-X
  1. Newbery Medal—Indexes. 2. Caldecott Medal—Indexes. 3. Children's literature, American—Indexes. 4. Picture books for children—United States—Indexes. I. Goetting, Denise.
Z1037.A2N465 2003
011.62—dc21

2003012891

Published by Linworth Publishing, Inc.
480 East Wilson Bridge Road, Suite L
Worthington, Ohio 43085

Copyright © 2003 by Linworth Publishing, Inc.

All rights reserved. Purchasing this book entitles a librarian to reproduce activity sheets for use in the library within a school or entitles a teacher to reproduce activity sheets for a single classroom use within a school. Other portions of the book (up to 15 pages) may be copied for staff development purposes within a single school. Standard citation information should appear on each page. The reproduction of any part of this book for an entire school or school system or for commercial use is strictly prohibited. No part of this book may be electronically reproduced, transmitted, or recorded without written permission from the publisher.

ISBN: 1-58683-083-X
5 4 3 2 1

Table of Contents

Introduction v

Subject Index to Newbery and Caldecott Books .. 1

Author/Illustrator Index 93

Title Index 97

About the Authors 103

Introduction

The first cries of "Help!" came from undergraduate students taking courses in children's literature to satisfy requirements for bachelor's degrees in elementary education. The next call came from university and college librarians assisting undergraduate students. Then the public and school librarians complained that elementary-age children also asked for Newbery and Caldecott titles relating to particular subjects, and further, that there were no reference books available to answer the demand. Although there were several books that annotated children's literature and indexed the titles by subject, there were none that indexed exclusively Newbery and Caldecott Award books by subject. This volume was created to meet this clear need for a subject index to all Newbery and Caldecott Award books.

This reference work provides the answers to such questions as: "Are there any Newbery titles dealing with presidents of the United States?" or "Which Caldecott books illustrate folk tales?" or "What are some Newbery Medal winners on topics such as the homeless or orphans?" The authors foresee that this subject index will fill a void in all reference collections which deal with children's literature. Our objective is to answer the cries for help from librarians, teachers, parents, and students seeking subject access to the Newbery and Caldecott Award books.

Of course, the reason that the Newbery and Caldecott titles are so important to librarians, teachers, and students is that these books are the "cream of the crop" of children's literature. Each year the Association for Library Service to Children (ALSC), a division of the American Library Association, awards a Newbery Medal to an American children's book for excellence in writing and a Caldecott Medal to an American children's picture book for quality of illustrations. Both fiction and nonfiction works are included in the awards. In most years runner-up books in each category are presented with honor awards. Newbery titles were first awarded in 1922, and Caldecott titles, in 1938. Since that time, 622 titles have received these recognitions of merit.

The contributors determined the need for this unique index because the Newbery and Caldecott titles stay in print longer than other children's books. Also, these works are in high demand by librarians, teachers, and students of all levels. As librarians with diverse library backgrounds, we have seen first hand the frustration of those seeking subject access to these titles. All four of the contributors have worked in public libraries, while three of us have served in school libraries. Two of us have taught children's literature classes at the university and community college levels. Through our experiences, we have witnessed the demand for a Newbery and Caldecott Awards index in public libraries, school libraries, and on the college level.

The book is arranged in alphabetical order by subject heading. Each entry includes author, title, and date of the award, with Caldecott entries additionally listing the illustrator if the author and illustrator are different. To distinguish between Newbery and Caldecott titles, the letters *N* or *C* follow the entry in brackets. A further differentiation with the letters *A* or *H* notes whether the book has been chosen as an award winner or honor title. Those titles that have won both Newbery and Caldecott prizes include both designations.

Subject headings assigned are based on the *Library of Congress Subject Headings*, specifically the Library of Congress *Subject Headings for Children's Literature* and *Subject Headings for Children: A List of Subject Headings Used by the Library of Congress with Abridged Dewey Numbers Added* (Albany, NY: Forest Press, 1998) edited by Lois Winkel. Headings are derived from the *Library of Congress Online Catalog* <http://catalog.loc.gov>, from Cataloging in Publication information, and from original cataloging. *Library of Congress Authorities* online, <http://authorities.loc.gov>, has been used to verify headings.

Literary genre headings such as historical fiction, mystery fiction, and adventure fiction, as well as form headings, such as biography and poetry, are incorporated. These headings have been validated in the LC online authorities and in *Guidelines on Subject Access to Individual Works of Fiction, Drama, Etc.* (Chicago: Resources and Technical Services Division, American Library Association, 2000).

Although the authors have attempted to be accurate and inclusive in choices of subject headings, readers may find errors or omissions. We quickly realized that earlier nonfiction works were cataloged with few subject headings, while earlier fiction titles were not assigned *any* subject headings. Therefore, for most of the pre-1980s fiction titles, we produced original cataloging. This made our project much more challenging and interesting. Because we propose to update this work periodically, we welcome suggestions for additions and improvements to future editions.

Subject Index to Newbery and Caldecott Books

Accidents—Fiction
Bauer, Marion Dane. *On My Honor.* [NH 1987]

Accidents—Prevention—Fiction
Rathmann, Peggy. *Officer Buckle and Gloria.* [CA 1996]

Adventure—Fiction
Babbitt, Natalie. *Knee Knock Rise.* [NH 1971]

Best, Herbert. *Garram the Hunter: A Boy of the Hill Tribes.* [NH 1931]

Bowen, William. *The Old Tobacco Shop.* [NH 1922]

du Bois, William Pène. *The Twenty-One Balloons.* [NA 1948]

Fisher, Cyrus, pseud. (Darwin L. Teilhet). *The Avion My Uncle Flew.* [NH 1947]

Fleischman, Sid. *The Whipping Boy.* [NA 1987]

George, Jean Craighead. *My Side of the Mountain.* [NH 1960]

Hiaasen, Carl. *Hoot.* [NH 2003]

Lide, Alice Alison. *Ood-le-uk the Wanderer.* [NH 1931]

O'Dell, Scott. *The Black Pearl.* [NH 1968]

O'Dell, Scott. *Island of the Blue Dolphins.* [NA 1961]

Rankin, Louise. *Daughter of the Mountains.* [NH 1949]

Sperry, Armstrong. *Call It Courage.* [NA 1941]

Tietjens, Eunice. *Boy of the South Seas.* [NH 1932]

Weil, Ann. *Red Sails to Capri.* [NH 1953]

Weston, Christine. *Bhimsa, the Dancing Bear.* [NH 1946]

Aeronautics
Freedman, Russell. *The Wright Brothers: How They Invented the Airplane.* [NH 1992]

Africa—Fiction
Farmer, Nancy. *The Ear, the Eye, and the Arm.* [NH 1995]

Farmer, Nancy. *A Girl Named Disaster.* [NH 1997]

Africa—Folklore
Courlander, Harold. *The Cow-Tail Switch, and Other West African Stories.* [NH 1948]

Dayrell, Elphinstone. *Why the Sun and the Moon Live in the Sky: A Nigerian Tale.* Illus. by Blair Lent. [CH 1969]

Grifalconi, Ann. *The Village of Round and Square Houses.* [CH 1987]

Haley, Gail E. *A Story A Story: An African Tale.* [CA 1971]

McDermott, Gerald. *Anansi the Spider: A Tale from the Ashanti.* [CH 1973]

Steptoe, John. *Mufaro's Beautiful Daughters: An African Tale.* [CH 1988]

Africa—Kings and rulers—Fiction

Best, Herbert. *Garram the Hunter: A Boy of the Hill Tribes*. **[NH 1931]**

Africa—Poetry

Cendrars, Blaise. *Shadow*. Illus. and trans. by Marcia Brown. **[CA 1983]**

Africa—Social life and customs

Musgrove, Margaret. *Ashanti to Zulu: African Traditions*. Illus. by Leo & Diane Dillon. **[CA 1977]**

Africa—Social life and customs—Folklore

Grifalconi, Ann. *The Village of Round and Square Houses*. **[CH 1987]**

Africa, East—Social life and customs

Feelings, Muriel. *Jambo Means Hello: Swahili Alphabet Book*. Illus. by Tom Feelings. **[CH 1975]**

Feelings, Muriel. *Moja Means One: Swahili Counting Book*. Illus. by Tom Feelings. **[CH 1972]**

Africa, West—Folklore

Aardema, Verna. *Why Mosquitoes Buzz in People's Ears: A West African Tale*. Illus. by Leo & Diane Dillon. **[CA 1976]**

African American agriculturists—Poetry

Nelson, Marilyn. *Carver: A Life in Poems*. **[NH 2002]**

African Americans—Biography

Pinkney, Andrea Davis. *Duke Ellington: The Piano Prince and the Orchestra*. Illus. by Brian Pinkney. **[CH 1999]**

Rappaport, Doreen. *Martin's Big Words: The Life of Dr. Martin Luther King, Jr.* Illus. by Bryan Collier. **[CH 2002]**

Yates, Elizabeth. *Amos Fortune, Free Man*. **[NA 1951]**

African Americans—Fiction

Brooks, Bruce. *The Moves Make the Man*. **[NH 1985]**

Fenner, Carol. *Yolonda's Genius*. **[NH 1996]**

Greene, Bette. *Philip Hall Likes Me, I Reckon Maybe*. **[NH 1975]**

Hamilton, Virginia. *M. C. Higgins, the Great*. **[NA 1975]**

Hamilton, Virginia. *The Planet of Junior Brown*. **[NH 1972]**

Hamilton, Virginia. *Sweet Whispers, Brother Rush*. **[NH 1983]**

Keats, Ezra Jack. *Goggles!* **[CH 1970]**

Keats, Ezra Jack. *The Snowy Day*. **[CA 1963]**

Konigsburg, E. L. *Jennifer, Hecate, Macbeth, William McKinley, and Me, Elizabeth*. **[NH 1968]**

Mathis, Sharon Bell. *The Hundred Penny Box*. **[NH 1976]**

McKissack, Patricia. *The Dark-Thirty: Southern Tales of the Supernatural*. **[NH 1993]**

McKissack, Patricia C. *Mirandy and Brother Wind*. Illus. by Jerry Pinkney. **[CH 1989]**

Myers, Walter Dean. *Scorpions*. **[NH 1989]**

Raschka, Christopher. *Yo! Yes?* **[CH 1994]**

Ringgold, Faith. *Tar Beach*. **[CH 1992]**

Weik, Mary Hays. *The Jazz Man*. **[NH 1967]**

Williams, Sherley Anne. *Working Cotton*. Illus. by Carole Byard. [CH 1993]

African Americans—Folklore

Lester, Julius. *John Henry*. Illus. by Jerry Pinkney. [CH 1995]

San Souci, Robert D. *The Talking Eggs: A Folktale from the American South*. Illus. by Jerry Pinkney. [CH 1990]

Stevens, Janet. *Tops & Bottoms*. [CH 1996]

African Americans—History

Bontemps, Arna. *Story of the Negro*. [NH 1949]

Lester, Julius. *To Be a Slave*. [NH 1969]

African Americans—History—Fiction

Armstrong, William H. *Sounder*. [NA 1970]

Curtis, Christopher Paul. *Bud, Not Buddy*. [NA 2000]

Curtis, Christopher Paul. *The Watsons Go to Birmingham—1963*. [NH 1996]

Swift, Hildegarde Hoyt. *The Railroad to Freedom: A Story of the Civil War*. [NH 1933]

Taylor, Mildred D. *Roll of Thunder, Hear My Cry*. [NA 1977]

African Americans—Massachusetts—Biography

Yates, Elizabeth. *Amos Fortune, Free Man*. [NA 1951]

African Americans—Poetry

Myers, Walter Dean. *Harlem*. Illus. by Christopher Myers. [CH 1998]

Nelson, Marilyn. *Carver: A Life in Poems*. [NH 2002]

Agassiz, Louis, 1807–1873

Robinson, Mabel Louise. *Runner of the Mountain Tops: The Life of Louis Agassiz*. [NH 1940]

Aged—Fiction

Davis, Lavinia R. *The Wild Birthday Cake*. Illus. by Hildegard Woodward. [CH 1950]

Enright, Elizabeth. *Gone-Away Lake*. [NH 1958]

Goffstein, M. B. *Fish for Supper*. [CH 1977]

Mathis, Sharon Bell. *The Hundred Penny Box*. [NH 1976]

Miles, Miska. *Annie and the Old One*. [NH 1972]

Agriculturists—Poetry

Nelson, Marilyn. *Carver: A Life in Poems*. [NH 2002]

Air pilots—Biography

Provensen, Alice & Martin. *The Glorious Flight: Across the Channel with Louis Bleriot*. [CA 1984]

Airplanes

Freedman, Russell. *The Wright Brothers: How They Invented the Airplane*. [NH 1992]

Airplanes—Design and construction

Provensen, Alice & Martin. *The Glorious Flight: Across the Channel with Louis Bleriot*. [CA 1984]

Airplanes—Fiction

Yep, Laurence. *Dragonwings*. [NH 1976]

Alabama—Fiction

Curtis, Christopher Paul. *The Watsons Go to Birmingham—1963*. [NH 1996]

Alaska—Fiction
George, Jean Craighead. *Julie of the Wolves.* [NA 1973]

Lide, Alice Alison. *Ood-le-uk the Wanderer.* [NH 1931]

Alaska—Folklore
Sleator, William. *The Angry Moon.* Illus. by Blair Lent. [CH 1971]

Albania—History—Fiction
Miller, Elizabeth. *Pran of Albania.* [NH 1930]

Alcoholism—Fiction
Conly, Jane Leslie. *Crazy Lady.* [NH 1994]

Gantos, Jack. *Joey Pigza Loses Control.* [NH 2001]

Weik, Mary Hays. *The Jazz Man.* [NH 1967]

Alcott, Louisa May, 1832–1888
Meigs, Cornelia. *Invincible Louisa: The Story of the Author of Little Women.* [NA 1934]

Alphabet
Baskin, Hosea, Tobias, and Lisa. *Hosie's Alphabet.* Illus. by Leonard Baskin. [CH 1973]

Feelings, Muriel. *Jambo Means Hello: Swahili Alphabet Book.* Illus. by Tom Feelings. [CH 1975]

Johnson, Stephen T. *Alphabet City.* [CH 1996]

Lobel, Arnold. *On Market Street.* Illus. by Anita Lobel. [CH 1982]

MacDonald, Suse. *Alphabatics.* [CH 1987]

Musgrove, Margaret. *Ashanti to Zulu: African Traditions.* Illus. by Leo & Diane Dillon. [CA 1977]

Pelletier, David. *The Graphic Alphabet.* [CH 1997]

Petersham, Maud & Miska. *An American ABC.* [CH 1942]

Alphabet—Fiction
Parrish, Anne. *The Story of Appleby Capple.* [NH 1951]

Alphabet rhymes
Eichenberg, Fritz. *Ape in a Cape: An Alphabet of Odd Animals.* [CH 1953]

Gág, Wanda. *The ABC Bunny.* [NH 1934]

McGinley, Phyllis. *All Around the Town.* Illus. by Helen Stone. [CH 1949]

Alps—Fiction
Ullman, James Ramsey. *Banner in the Sky.* [NH 1955]

America—Antiquities
Baity, Elizabeth. *Americans Before Columbus.* [NH 1952]

America—Discovery and exploration
Johnson, Gerald W. *America Is Born: A History for Peter.* [NH 1960]

America—Discovery and exploration—Fiction
Colum, Padriac. *The Voyagers: Being Legends and Romances of Atlantic Discovery.* [NH 1926]

America—Discovery and exploration—Pre-Columbian
Baity, Elizabeth. *Americans Before Columbus.* [NH 1952]

American literature—History and criticism
Gurko, Leo. *Tom Paine, Freedom's Apostle.* [NH 1958]

Amish—Fiction
de Angeli, Marguerite. *Yonie Wondernose.* [CH 1945]

Amusement parks—Fiction
Ets, Marie Hall. *Mr. Penny's Race Horse.* [CH 1957]

Anansi (Legendary character)
McDermott, Gerald. *Anansi the Spider: A Tale from the Ashanti.* [CH 1973]

Anatole (Fictitious character)
Titus, Eve. *Anatole.* Illus. by Paul Galdone. [CH 1957]

Titus, Eve. *Anatole and the Cat.* Illus. by Paul Galdone. [CH 1958]

Andes Region—Fiction
Clark, Ann Nolan. *Secret of the Andes.* [NA 1953]

Androcles and the Lion (Fable)—Adaptations
Daugherty, James. *Andy and the Lion.* [CH 1939]

Angels—Fiction
du Bois, William Pène. *Lion.* [CH 1957]

Anger—Fiction
Bang, Molly. *When Sophie Gets Angry—Really, Really Angry.* [CH 2000]

Animal life cycles—Fiction
Holling, Holling C. *Minn of the Mississippi.* [NH 1952]

Schlein, Miriam. *When Will the World Be Mine?* Illus. by Jean Charlot. [CH 1954]

Yates, Elizabeth. *Mountain Born.* [NH 1944]

Animals
Eichenberg, Fritz. *Ape in a Cape: An Alphabet of Odd Animals.* [CH 1953]

Spier, Peter. *Noah's Ark.* [CA 1978]

Animals—Fiction
Armer, Laura Adams. *The Forest Pool.* [CH 1939]

de Regniers, Beatrice Schenk. *May I Bring a Friend?* Illus. by Beni Montresor. [CA 1965]

du Bois, William Pène. *Lion.* [CH 1957]

Ets, Marie Hall. *In the Forest.* [CH 1945]

Ets, Marie Hall. *Just Me.* [CH 1966]

Ets, Marie Hall. *Mr. Penny's Race Horse.* [CH 1957]

Ets, Marie Hall. *Mr. T. W. Anthony Woo.* [CH 1952]

Ets, Marie Hall. *Play with Me.* [CH 1956]

Gannett, Ruth S. *My Father's Dragon.* [NH 1949]

Hader, Berta & Elmer. *The Big Snow.* [CA 1949]

Krauss, Ruth. *The Happy Day.* Illus. by Marc Simon. [CH 1950]

Langstaff, John. *Frog Went-A-Courtin'.* Illus. by Fedor Rojankovsky. [CA 1956]

Lawson, Robert. *Rabbit Hill.* [NA 1945]

Lobel, Arnold. *Fables.* [CA 1981]

Lofting, Hugh. *The Voyages of Doctor Dolittle.* [NA 1923]

O'Brien, Robert C. *Mrs. Frisby and the Rats of NIMH.* [NA 1972]

Politi, Leo. *Juanita.* [CH 1949]

Rohmann, Eric. *My Friend Rabbit.* [CA 2003]

Animals—Folklore
Aardema, Verna. *Why Mosquitoes Buzz in People's Ears: A West African Tale.* Illus. by Leo & Diane Dillon. [CA 1976]

Plume, Ilse. *The Bremen-Town Musicians*. Adapted from the Brothers Grimm. **[CH 1981]**

Zemach, Margot. *It Could Always Be Worse: A Yiddish Tale*. **[CH 1978]**

Animals—Infancy—Fiction

Birnbaum, A. *Green Eyes*. **[CH 1954]**

Animals—Poetry

Seuss, Dr., pseud. (Theodor Seuss Geisel). *If I Ran the Zoo*. **[CH 1951]**

Willard, Nancy. *A Visit to William Blake's Inn: Poems for Innocent and Experienced Travelers*. **[NA 1982, CH 1982]**

Animals—Songs and music

Emberley, Barbara. *One Wide River to Cross*. Illus. by Ed Emberley. **[CH 1967]**

Animals—Treatment—Fiction

Naylor, Phyllis Reynolds. *Shiloh*. **[NA 1992]**

Animals—Wintering—Fiction

Lionni, Leo. *Frederick*. **[CH 1968]**

Animals in art

Baskin, Hosea, Tobias, and Lisa. *Hosie's Alphabet*. Illus. by Leonard Baskin. **[CH 1973]**

Ehlert, Lois. *Color Zoo*. **[CH 1990]**

Jeffers, Susan. *Three Jovial Huntsmen*. **[CH 1974]**

Animals in the Bible

Lathrop, Dorothy P. *Animals of the Bible, a Picture Book*. **[CA 1938]**

Anthropology

Van Loon, Hendrik Willem. *The Story of Mankind*. **[NA 1922]**

Apartment houses—Fiction

Newberry, Clare Turlay. *April's Kittens*. **[CH 1941]**

Appalachian Mountains—Fiction

Rylant, Cynthia. *When I Was Young in the Mountains*. Illus. by Diane Goode. **[CH 1983]**

Apple growers—Biography

Hunt, Mabel Leigh. *Better Known as Johnny Appleseed*. **[NH 1951]**

Apples—Fiction

Caudill, Rebecca. *Tree of Freedom*. **[NH 1950]**

Appleseed, Johnny, 1774–1845

Hunt, Mabel Leigh. *Better Known as Johnny Appleseed*. **[NH 1951]**

Apprentices—Fiction

Cushman, Karen. *The Midwife's Apprentice*. **[NA 1996]**

Forbes, Esther. *Johnny Tremain*. **[NA 1944]**

Kyle, Anne. *The Apprentice of Florence*. **[NH 1934]**

Arabian horse—Fiction

Henry, Marguerite. *King of the Wind*. **[NA 1949]**

Architecture—Medieval

Macaulay, David. *Castle*. **[CH 1978]**

Macaulay, David. *Cathedral*. **[CH 1974]**

Architecture, Gothic

Macaulay, David. *Cathedral*. **[CH 1974]**

Architecture in art

Johnson, Stephen T. *Alphabet City*. **[CH 1996]**

Argentina—Fiction
Kalnay, Francis. *Chucaro: Wild Pony of the Pampa.* [NH 1959]

Argonauts (Greek mythology)
Colum, Padraic. *The Golden Fleece and the Heroes Who Lived before Achilles.* [NH 1922]

Arkansas—Fiction
Greene, Bette. *Philip Hall Likes Me, I Reckon Maybe.* [NH 1975]

Armenia—Folklore
Hogrogian, Nonny. *The Contest.* [CH 1977]

Hogrogian, Nonny. *One Fine Day.* [CA 1972]

Armenians—Turkey—Biography
Kherdian, David. *The Road from Home: The Story of an Armenian Girl.* [NH 1980]

Art appreciation
Moore, Janet Gaylord. *The Many Ways of Seeing: An Introduction to the Pleasures of Art.* [NH 1970]

Art, Renaissance
Ford, Lauren. *The Ageless Story.* [CH 1940]

Arthur, King—Legends
Jewett, Eleanore. *The Hidden Treasure of Glaston.* [NH 1947]

Artists—Fiction
Coatsworth, Elizabeth. *The Cat Who Went to Heaven.* [NA 1931]

Giff, Patricia Reilly. *Pictures of Hollis Woods.* [NH 2003]

Shannon, Monica. *Dobry.* [NA 1935]

Trevino, Elizabeth Borton de. *I, Juan de Pareja.* [NA 1966]

Artists—Great Britain—Biography
Kerley, Barbara. *The Dinosaurs of Waterhouse Hawkins: An Illuminating History of Mr. Waterhouse Hawkins, Artist and Lecturer.* Illus. by Brian Selznick. [CH 2002]

Artists—United States—Biography
Rourke, Constance. *Audubon.* [NH 1937]

Ashanti (African people)—Folklore
McDermott, Gerald. *Anansi the Spider: A Tale from the Ashanti.* [CH 1973]

Astronomers—Biography
Sís, Peter. *Starry Messenger: A Book Depicting the Life of a Famous Scientist, Mathematician, Astronomer, Philosopher, Physicist, Galileo Galilei.* [CH 1997]

Astronomers—Fiction
Latham, Jean Lee. *Carry On, Mr. Bowditch.* [NA 1956]

Athletes—Fiction
Spinelli, Jerry. *Maniac Magee.* [NA 1991]

Attention-deficit hyperactivity disorder—Fiction
Gantos, Jack. *Joey Pigza Loses Control.* [NH 2001]

Audubon, John James, 1785–1851
Rourke, Constance. *Audubon.* [NH 1937]

Aunts—Fiction
Bauer, Joan. *Hope Was Here.* [NH 2001]

Couloumbis, Audrey. *Getting Near to Baby.* [NH 2000]

Hunt, Irene. *Up a Road Slowly.* [NA 1967]

Mathis, Sharon Bell. *The Hundred Penny Box.* [NH 1976]

Rylant, Cynthia. *Missing May.* [NA 1993]

Authors, American—19th century—Biography

Meigs, Cornelia. *Invincible Louisa: The Story of the Author of Little Women.* [NA 1934]

Authors, American—20th century—Biography

de Paola, Tomie. *26 Fairmount Avenue.* [NH 2000]

Peet, Bill. *Bill Peet: An Autobiography.* [CH 1990]

B

Babies—Fiction

Couloumbis, Audrey. *Getting Near to Baby.* [NH 2000]

Newberry, Clare Turlay. *T-Bone, the Baby Sitter.* [CH 1951]

Sendak, Maurice. *Outside Over There.* [CH 1982]

Williams, Vera B. *"More More More," Said the Baby: Three Love Stories.* [CH 1991]

Babysitters—Fiction

Newberry, Clare Turlay. *T-Bone, the Baby Sitter.* [CH 1951]

Badgers—Fiction

Eckert, Allan W. *Incident at Hawk's Hill.* [NH 1972]

Bagpipes—Fiction

Leaf, Munro. *Wee Gillis.* Illus. by Robert Lawson. [CH 1939]

Baking—Fiction

Sendak, Maurice. *In the Night Kitchen.* [CH 1971]

Ballads—England

Malcolmson, Anne, editor. *Song of Robin Hood.* Designed and illus. by Virginia Lee Burton. [CH 1948]

Ballads—United States

Thayer, Ernest Lawrence. *Casey at the Bat: A Ballad of the Republic Sung in the Year 1888.* Illus. by Christopher Bing. [CH 2001]

Balloons—Fiction

du Bois, William Pène. *The Twenty-One Balloons.* [NA 1948]

Baptists—United States—Clergy—Biography

Rappaport, Doreen. *Martin's Big Words: The Life of Dr. Martin Luther King, Jr.* Illus. by Bryan Collier. [CH 2002]

Baseball—Fiction

Gantos, Jack. *Joey Pigza Loses Control.* [NH 2001]

Baseball—Poetry

Thayer, Ernest Lawrence. *Casey at the Bat: A Ballad of the Republic Sung in the Year 1888.* Illus. by Christopher Bing. [CH 2001]

Bashfulness—Fiction

Yashima, Taro. *Crow Boy.* [CH 1956]

Basketball—Fiction

Brooks, Bruce. *The Moves Make the Man.* [NH 1985]

Baths—Fiction

Wood, Audrey. *King Bidgood's in the Bathtub.* Illus. by Don Wood. [CH 1986]

Batting (Baseball)—Poetry

Thayer, Ernest Lawrence. *Casey at the Bat: A Ballad of the Republic Sung in the Year 1888*. Illus. by Christopher Bing. **[CH 2001]**

Beaches—Fiction

Giff, Patricia Reilly. *Lily's Crossing*. **[NH 1998]**

McCloskey, Robert. *One Morning in Maine*. **[CH 1953]**

Beans—Fiction

Brown, Marcia. *Skipper John's Cook*. **[CH 1952]**

Bears—Fiction

Dalgliesh, Alice. *The Bears on Hemlock Mountain*. **[NH 1953]**

du Bois, William Pène. *Bear Party*. **[CH 1952]**

Jarrell, Randall. *The Animal Family*. **[NH 1966]**

McCloskey, Robert. *Blueberries for Sal*. **[CH 1949]**

Minarik, Else H. *Little Bear's Visit*. Illus. by Maurice Sendak. **[CH 1962]**

Ward, Lynd. *The Biggest Bear*. **[CA 1953]**

Weston, Christine. *Bhimsa, the Dancing Bear*. **[NH 1946]**

Bears—Folklore

Marshall, James. *Goldilocks and the Three Bears*. **[CH 1989]**

Stevens, Janet. *Tops & Bottoms*. **[CH 1996]**

Bedtime—Fiction

Bang, Molly. *Ten, Nine, Eight*. **[CH 1984]**

Brown, Margaret Wise. *A Child's Good Night Book*. Illus. by Jean Charlot. **[CH 1944]**

Beekeepers—Fiction

Meigs, Cornelia. *The Windy Hill*. **[NH 1922]**

Behavior—Fiction

Bauer, Marion Dane. *On My Honor*. **[NH 1987]**

Falconer, Ian. *Olivia*. **[CH 2001]**

Kepes, Juliet. *Five Little Monkeys*. **[CH 1953]**

Newberry, Clare Turlay. *T-Bone, the Baby Sitter*. **[CH 1951]**

Shannon, David. *No, David!* **[CH 1999]**

Will, pseud. (William Lipkind). *The Two Reds*. Illus. by Nicolas, pseud. (Nicolas Mordvinoff). **[CH 1951]**

Bentley, W. A. (Wilson Alwyn), 1865–1931

Martin, Jacqueline Briggs. *Snowflake Bentley*. Illus. by Mary Azarian. **[CA 1999]**

Berehove (Ukraine)—Biography

Siegal, Aranka. *Upon the Head of the Goat: A Childhood in Hungary, 1939–1944*. **[NH 1982]**

Berehove (Ukraine)—Ethnic relations

Siegal, Aranka. *Upon the Head of the Goat: A Childhood in Hungary, 1939–1944*. **[NH 1982]**

Bible—Natural history

Lathrop, Dorothy P. *Animals of the Bible, a Picture Book*. **[CA 1938]**

Bible stories

Jones, Jessie Orton. *Small Rain: Verses from the Bible*. Illus. by Elizabeth Orton Jones. **[CH 1944]**

Bible stories O.T. Genesis
Pinkney, Jerry. *Noah's Ark.* **[CH 2003]**
Spier, Peter. *Noah's Ark.* **[CA 1978]**

Biography
Coolidge, Olivia. *Men of Athens.* **[NH 1963]**
d'Aulaire, Ingri & Edgar Parin. *Abraham Lincoln.* **[CA 1940]**
Daugherty, James. *Daniel Boone.* **[NA 1940]**
de Paola, Tomie. *26 Fairmount Avenue.* **[NH 2000]**
Eaton, Jeanette. *A Daughter of the Seine: The Life of Madame Roland.* **[NH 1930]**
Eaton, Jeanette. *Gandhi, Fighter without a Sword.* **[NH 1951]**
Eaton, Jeanette. *Leader by Destiny: George Washington, Man and Patriot.* **[NH 1939]**
Eaton, Jeanette. *Lone Journey: The Life of Roger Williams.* **[NH 1945]**
Foster, Genevieve. *Abraham Lincoln's World.* **[NH 1945]**
Foster, Genevieve. *George Washington.* **[NH 1950]**
Foster, Genevieve. *George Washington's World.* **[NH 1942]**
Freedman, Russell. *Eleanor Roosevelt: A Life of Discovery.* **[NH 1994]**
Freedman, Russell. *Lincoln: A Photobiography.* **[NA 1988]**
Freedman, Russell. *The Wright Brothers: How They Invented the Airplane.* **[NH 1992]**
Gray, Elizabeth Janet (Elizabeth Gray Vining). *Penn.* **[NH 1939]**
Gurko, Leo. *Tom Paine, Freedom's Apostle.* **[NH 1958]**
Hall, Anna Gertrude. *Nansen.* **[NH 1941]**
Holbrook, Stewart. *America's Ethan Allen.* Illus. by Lynd Ward. **[CH 1950]**
Hunt, Mabel Leigh. *Better Known as Johnny Appleseed.* **[NH 1951]**
Hunt, Mabel Leigh. *"Have You Seen Tom Thumb?"* **[NH 1943]**
Judson, Clara Ingram. *Abraham Lincoln, Friend of the People.* **[NH 1951]**
Judson, Clara Ingram. *Mr. Justice Holmes.* **[NH 1957]**
Judson, Clara Ingram. *Theodore Roosevelt, Fighting Patriot.* **[NH 1954]**
Kerley, Barbara. *The Dinosaurs of Waterhouse Hawkins: An Illuminating History of Mr. Waterhouse Hawkins, Artist and Lecturer.* Illus. by Brian Selznick. **[CH 2002]**
Kherdian, David. *The Road from Home: The Story of an Armenian Girl.* **[NH 1980]**
Lawson, Robert. *They Were Strong and Good.* **[CA 1941]**
Martin, Jacqueline Briggs. *Snowflake Bentley.* Illus. by Mary Azarian. **[CA 1999]**
Meigs, Cornelia. *Invincible Louisa: The Story of the Author of Little Women.* **[NA 1934]**
North, Sterling. *Rascal: A Memoir of a Better Era.* **[NH 1964]**
Peet, Bill. *Bill Peet: An Autobiography.* **[CH 1990]**
Pinkney, Andrea Davis. *Duke Ellington: The Piano Prince and the Orchestra.* Illus. by Brian Pinkney. **[CH 1999]**
Provensen, Alice & Martin. *The Glorious Flight: Across the Channel with Louis Bleriot.* **[CA 1984]**

Rappaport, Doreen. *Martin's Big Words: The Life of Dr. Martin Luther King, Jr.* Illus. by Bryan Collier. **[CH 2002]**

Reiss, Johanna. *The Upstairs Room.* **[NH 1973]**

Robinson, Mabel Louise. *Runner of the Mountain Tops: The Life of Louis Agassiz.* **[NH 1940]**

Rourke, Constance. *Audubon.* **[NH 1937]**

Rourke, Constance. *Davy Crockett.* **[NH 1935]**

Shippen, Katherine B. *Men, Microscopes, and Living Things.* **[NH 1956]**

Siegal, Aranka. *Upon the Head of the Goat: A Childhood in Hungary, 1939–1944.* **[NH 1982]**

Sís, Peter. *Starry Messenger: A Book Depicting the Life of a Famous Scientist, Mathematician, Astronomer, Philosopher, Physicist, Galileo Galilei.* **[CH 1997]**

St. George, Judith. *So You Want to Be President?* Illus. by David Small. **[CA 2001]**

Yates, Elizabeth. *Amos Fortune, Free Man.* **[NA 1951]**

Biologists—Biography

Shippen, Katherine B. *Men, Microscopes, and Living Things.* **[NH 1956]**

Biology—History

Shippen, Katherine B. *Men, Microscopes, and Living Things.* **[NH 1956]**

Birds—Fiction

Lionni, Leo. *Inch by Inch.* **[CH 1961]**

Olds, Elizabeth. *Feather Mountain.* **[CH 1952]**

Rohmann, Eric. *Time Flies.* **[CH 1995]**

Yorinks, Arthur. *Hey, Al.* Illus. by Richard Egielski. **[CA 1987]**

Birds—Migration—Fiction

Brown, Margaret Wise. *Wheel on the Chimney.* Illus. by Tibor Gergely. **[CH 1955]**

Birds—Nests—Fiction

Freeman, Don. *Fly High, Fly Low.* **[CH 1958]**

Birds in art

Rourke, Constance. *Audubon.* **[NH 1937]**

Birthdays—Fiction

Davis, Lavinia R. *The Wild Birthday Cake.* Illus. by Hildegard Woodward. **[CH 1950]**

Bison—Fiction

Baker, Olaf. *Where the Buffaloes Begin.* Illus. by Stephen Gammell. **[CH 1982]**

Black race—History

Bontemps, Arna. *Story of the Negro.* **[NH 1949]**

Blacks—Zimbabwe—Fiction

Farmer, Nancy. *The Ear, the Eye, and the Arm.* **[NH 1995]**

Blake, William, 1757–1827—Poetry

Willard, Nancy. *A Visit to William Blake's Inn: Poems for Innocent and Experienced Travelers.* **[NA 1982, CH 1982]**

Blankets—Fiction

Henkes, Kevin. *Owen.* **[CH 1994]**

Blériot, Louis, 1872–1936
Provensen, Alice & Martin. *The Glorious Flight: Across the Channel with Louis Bleriot.* [CA 1984]

Blind—Folklore
Young, Ed. *Seven Blind Mice.* [CH 1993]

Blizzards—Fiction
Wilder, Laura Ingalls. *The Long Winter.* [NH 1941]

Blue Grotto (Italy)—Fiction
Weil, Ann. *Red Sails to Capri.* [NH 1953]

Blueberries—Fiction
McCloskey, Robert. *Blueberries for Sal.* [CH 1949]

Boarding schools—Fiction
Bemelmans, Ludwig. *Madeline.* [CH 1940]

Bemelmans, Ludwig. *Madeline's Rescue.* [CA 1954]

Boats and boating—Fiction
Flack, Marjorie. *Boats on the River.* Illus. by Jay Hyde Barnum. [CH 1947]

Bones—Fiction
Steig, William. *The Amazing Bone.* [CH 1977]

Will, pseud. (William Lipkind). *Finders Keepers.* Illus. by Nicolas, pseud. (Nicolas Mordvinoff). [CA 1952]

Boone, Daniel, 1734–1820
Daugherty, James. *Daniel Boone.* [NA 1940]

Boredom—Fiction
Van Allsburg, Chris. *Jumanji.* [CA 1982]

Boston (England)—History—To 1500—Fiction
Whitney, Elinor. *Tod of the Fens.* [NH 1929]

Boston (Mass.)—Fiction
Hewes, Agnes Danforth. *Glory of the Seas.* [NH 1934]

McCloskey, Robert. *Make Way for Ducklings.* [CA 1942]

Boston (Mass.)—History—Revolution, 1775–1783—Fiction
Forbes, Esther. *Johnny Tremain.* [NA 1944]

Boston Tea Party, 1773—Fiction
Forbes, Esther. *Johnny Tremain.* [NA 1944]

British Columbia—Fiction
Horvath, Polly. *Everything on a Waffle.* [NH 2002]

Brothers—Fiction
Collier, James Lincoln & Christopher. *My Brother Sam Is Dead.* [NH 1975]

Hubbard, Ralph. *Queer Person.* [NH 1931]

Brothers—Folklore
Artzybasheff, Boris. *Seven Simeons: A Russian Tale.* [CH 1938]

Brothers and sisters—Fiction
Bartone, Elisa. *Peppe the Lamplighter.* Illus. by Ted Lewin. [CH 1994]

Bianco, Margery Williams. *Winterbound.* [NH 1937]

Brink, Carol Ryrie. *Caddie Woodlawn.* [NA 1936]

Byars, Betsy. *Summer of the Swans.* [NA 1971]

Curtis, Christopher Paul. *The Watsons Go to Birmingham—1963.* **[NH 1996]**

Enright, Elizabeth. *Thimble Summer.* **[NA 1939]**

Estes, Eleanor. *Ginger Pye.* **[NA 1952]**

Estes, Eleanor. *Rufus M.* **[NH 1944]**

Fenner, Carol. *Yolonda's Genius.* **[NH 1996]**

Handforth, Thomas. *Mei Li.* **[CA 1939]**

Henry, Marguerite. *Misty of Chincoteague.* **[NH 1948]**

Holm, Jennifer L. *Our Only May Amelia.* **[NH 2000]**

Konigsburg, E. L. *From the Mixed-Up Files of Mrs. Basil E. Frankweiler.* **[NA 1968]**

Meigs, Cornelia. *The Windy Hill.* **[NH 1922]**

Newberry, Clare Turlay. *April's Kittens.* **[CH 1941]**

Newberry, Clare Turlay. *Barkis.* **[CH 1939]**

Voigt, Cynthia. *Dicey's Song.* **[NA 1983]**

Bruges (Belgium)—Fiction

Bemelmans, Ludwig. *The Golden Basket.* **[NH 1937]**

Buddhism—Fiction

Coatsworth, Elizabeth. *The Cat Who Went to Heaven.* **[NA 1931]**

Bulgaria—Fiction

Shannon, Monica. *Dobry.* **[NA 1935]**

Bullfights—Fiction

Wojciechowska, Maia. *Shadow of a Bull.* **[NA 1965]**

Bullies—Fiction

Keats, Ezra Jack. *Goggles!* **[CH 1970]**

Buried treasure—Fiction

Sachar, Louis. *Holes.* **[NA 1999]**

Burrowing owl—Fiction

Hiaasen, Carl. *Hoot.* **[NH 2003]**

Butterflies—Fiction

Parrish, Anne. *The Story of Appleby Capple.* **[NH 1951]**

C

Cakes—Fiction

Sawyer, Ruth. *The Christmas Anna Angel.* Illus. by Kate Seredy. **[CH 1945]**

California—Fiction

Buff, Mary & Conrad. *Big Tree.* **[NH 1947]**

Montgomery, Rutherford. *Kildee House.* **[NH 1950]**

Politi, Leo. *Song of the Swallows.* **[CA 1950]**

Schaefer, Jack. *Old Ramon.* **[NH 1961]**

Snyder, Zilpha Keatley. *The Egypt Game.* **[NH 1968]**

Snyder, Zilpha Keatley. *The Witches of Worm.* **[NH 1973]**

Camels—Fiction

Staples, Suzanne Fisher. *Shabanu, Daughter of the Wind.* **[NH 1990]**

Cameroon—Folklore

Grifalconi, Ann. *The Village of Round and Square Houses.* **[CH 1987]**

Canada—Farm life—Fiction

Eckert, Allan W. *Incident at Hawk's Hill.* **[NH 1972]**

Canada—Fiction

Holling, Holling C. *Paddle-to-the-Sea.* **[CH 1942]**

Kingman, Lee. *Pierre Pidgeon*. Illus. by Arnold E. Bare. **[CH 1944]**

Paulsen, Gary. *Hatchet*. **[NH 1988]**

Canada goose—Fiction

Langton, Jane. *The Fledgling*. **[NH 1981]**

Cancer—Fiction

Bauer, Joan. *Hope Was Here*. **[NH 2001]**

Mazer, Norma Fox. *After the Rain*. **[NH 1988]**

Canoes—Fiction

Holling, Holling C. *Paddle-to-the-Sea*. **[CH 1942]**

Cape Cod (Mass.)—Fiction

Tresselt, Alvin. *Hide and Seek Fog*. Illus. by Roger Duvoisin. **[CH 1966]**

Cape Horn (Chile)—Fiction

Sperry, Armstrong. *All Sail Set: A Romance of the Flying Cloud*. **[NH 1936]**

Cape of Good Hope (South Africa)—History—Fiction

Hewes, Agnes Danforth. *Spice and the Devil's Cave*. **[NH 1931]**

Capri Island (Italy)—Fiction

Weil, Ann. *Red Sails to Capri*. **[NH 1953]**

Cartoonists—Biography

Peet, Bill. *Bill Peet: An Autobiography*. **[CH 1990]**

Carver, George Washington, 1864–1943—Poetry

Nelson, Marilyn. *Carver: A Life in Poems*. **[NH 2002]**

Casey, Brian Kavanagh, 1859–1946—Poetry

Thayer, Ernest Lawrence. *Casey at the Bat: A Ballad of the Republic Sung in the Year 1888*. Illus. by Christopher Bing. **[CH 2001]**

Castles

Macaulay, David. *Castle*. **[CH 1978]**

Castles—Fiction

Pope, Elizabeth Marie. *The Perilous Gard*. **[NH 1975]**

Cathedrals

Macaulay, David. *Cathedral*. **[CH 1974]**

Cats—Fiction

Birnbaum, A. *Green Eyes*. **[CH 1954]**

Bunting, Eve. *Smoky Night*. Illus. by David Diaz. **[CA 1995]**

Coatsworth, Elizabeth. *The Cat Who Went to Heaven*. **[NA 1931]**

Coblentz, Catherine. *The Blue Cat of Castle Town*. **[NH 1950]**

Fox, Paula. *One-Eyed Cat*. **[NH 1985]**

Gág, Wanda. *Millions of Cats*. **[NH 1929]**

Low, Joseph. *Mice Twice*. **[CH 1981]**

MacDonald, Golden, pseud. (Margaret Wise Brown). *The Little Island*. Illus. by Leonard Weisgard. **[CA 1947]**

McCarty, Peter. *Hondo & Fabian*. **[CH 2003]**

Neville, Emily. *It's Like This, Cat*. **[NA 1964]**

Newberry, Clare Turlay. *April's Kittens*. **[CH 1941]**

Newberry, Clare Turlay. *Barkis*. **[CH 1939]**

Newberry, Clare Turlay. *Marshmallow.* [CH 1943]

Newberry, Clare Turlay. *T-Bone, the Baby Sitter.* [CH 1951]

Selden, George, pseud. (George Thompson). *The Cricket in Times Square.* [NH 1961]

Snyder, Zilpha Keatley. *The Witches of Worm.* [NH 1973]

Titus, Eve. *Anatole and the Cat.* Illus. by Paul Galdone. [CH 1958]

Will, pseud. (William Lipkind). *The Two Reds.* Illus. by Nicolas, pseud. (Nicolas Mordvinoff). [CH 1951]

Cats—Folklore

Brown, Marcia. *Dick Whittington and His Cat.* [CH 1951]

Brown, Marcia. *Puss in Boots.* Adapted from Charles Perrault. [CH 1953]

Marcellino, Fred. *Puss in Boots.* Trans. by Malcolm Arthur; adapted from Charles Perrault. [CH 1991]

Caves—Fiction

Weil, Ann. *Red Sails to Capri.* [NH 1953]

Celts—Folklore

Young, Ella. *The Tangle-Coated Horse and Other Tales.* [NH 1930]

Chairs—Fiction

Williams, Vera B. *A Chair for My Mother.* [CH 1983]

Characters in literature—Fiction

Wiesner, David. *The Three Pigs.* [CA 2002]

Cheese—Fiction

Titus, Eve. *Anatole.* Illus. by Paul Galdone. [CH 1957]

Chesapeake Bay Region (Md. and Va.)—Fiction

Paterson, Katherine. *Jacob Have I Loved.* [NA 1981]

Voigt, Cynthia. *Dicey's Song.* [NA 1983]

Cheyenne Indians—Fiction

Sandoz, Mari. *The Horsecatcher.* [NH 1958]

Chicago (Ill.)—History—To 1875

Murphy, Jim. *The Great Fire.* [NH 1996]

Chickens—Fiction

DeJong, Meindert. *Along Came a Dog.* [NH 1959]

Hader, Berta & Elmer. *Cock-a-Doodle Doo.* [CH 1940]

Child abuse—Fiction

Coman, Carolyn. *What Jamie Saw.* [NH 1996]

Child labor—Fiction

Williams, Sherley Anne. *Working Cotton.* Illus. by Carole Byard. [CH 1993]

Childbirth—Fiction

Cushman, Karen. *The Midwife's Apprentice.* [NA 1996]

Children—Biography

de Paola, Tomie. *26 Fairmount Avenue.* [NH 2000]

Kherdian, David. *The Road from Home: The Story of an Armenian Girl.* [NH 1980]

North, Sterling. *Rascal: A Memoir of a Better Era.* [NH 1964]

Reiss, Johanna. *The Upstairs Room.* [NH 1973]

Siegal, Aranka. *Upon the Head of the Goat: A Childhood in Hungary, 1939–1944.* [NH 1982]

Children and the aged—Fiction

Ackerman, Karen. *Song and Dance Man.* Illus. by Stephen Gammell. [CA 1989]

Creech, Sharon. *Walk Two Moons.* [NA 1995]

Davis, Lavinia R. *The Wild Birthday Cake.* Illus. by Hildegard Woodward. [CH 1950]

Enright, Elizabeth. *Gone-Away Lake.* [NH 1958]

Giff, Patricia Reilly. *Pictures of Hollis Woods.* [NH 2003]

L'Engle, Madeleine. *A Ring of Endless Light.* [NH 1981]

Mathis, Sharon Bell. *The Hundred Penny Box.* [NH 1976]

Mazer, Norma Fox. *After the Rain.* [NH 1988]

Miles, Miska. *Annie and the Old One.* [NH 1972]

Minarik, Else H. *Little Bear's Visit.* Illus. by Maurice Sendak. [CH 1962]

Peck, Richard. *A Long Way from Chicago.* [NH 1999]

Peck, Richard. *A Year Down Yonder.* [NA 2001]

Voigt, Cynthia. *Dicey's Song.* [NA 1983]

Chimneys—Fiction

Brown, Margaret Wise. *Wheel on the Chimney.* Illus. by Tibor Gergely. [CH 1955]

China—Description and travel

Sís, Peter. *Tibet: Through the Red Box.* [CH 1999]

China—Fiction

Chrisman, Arthur Bowie. *Shen of the Sea.* [NA 1926]

Fritz, Jean and Margot Tomes. *Homesick: My Own Story.* [NH 1983]

Lewis, Elizabeth Foreman. *Young Fu of the Upper Yangtze.* [NA 1933]

Rankin, Louise. *Daughter of the Mountains.* [NH 1949]

Treffinger, Carolyn. *Li Lun, Lad of Courage.* [NH 1948]

Wiese, Kurt. *Fish in the Air.* [CH 1949]

China—Folklore

Chan, Chih-Yi. *Good-Luck Horse.* Illus. by Plato Chan. [CH 1944]

Yolen, Jane. *The Emperor and the Kite.* Illus. by Ed Young. [CH 1968]

Young, Ed. *Lon Po Po: A Red-Riding Hood Story from China.* [CA 1990]

China—History

Seeger, Elizabeth. *The Pageant of Chinese History.* [NH 1935]

China—History—1937–1945—Fiction

DeJong, Meindert. *The House of Sixty Fathers.* [NH 1957]

China—Social life and customs—Fiction

Handforth, Thomas. *Mei Li.* [CA 1939]

Chincoteague Island (Va.)—Fiction

Henry, Marguerite. *Misty of Chincoteague.* [NH 1948]

Chincoteague pony—Fiction
Henry, Marguerite. *Misty of Chincoteague.* **[NH 1948]**

Chinese Americans—Fiction
Yep, Laurence. *Dragonwings.* **[NH 1976]**

Chinese Americans—History—Fiction
Yep, Laurence. *Dragon's Gate.* **[NH 1994]**

Chinese language—Writing
Wiese, Kurt. *You Can Write Chinese.* **[CH 1946]**

Cholistan Desert (Pakistan)—Fiction
Staples, Suzanne Fisher. *Shabanu, Daughter of the Wind.* **[NH 1990]**

Christianity—Fiction
Speare, Elizabeth George. *The Bronze Bow.* **[NA 1962]**

Christianity—Latin America
Shippen, Katherine. *New Found World.* **[NH 1946]**

Christmas—Fiction
Ets, Marie Hall and Aurora Labastida. *Nine Days to Christmas.* Illus. by Marie Hall Ets. **[CA 1960]**

Politi, Leo. *Pedro, the Angel of Olvera Street.* **[CH 1947]**

Robbins, Ruth. *Baboushka and the Three Kings.* Illus. by Nicolas Sidjakov. **[CA 1961]**

Sauer, Julia. *The Light at Tern Rock.* **[NH 1952]**

Van Allsburg, Chris. *The Polar Express.* **[CA 1986]**

Christmas—Hungary—Fiction
Sawyer, Ruth. *The Christmas Anna Angel.* Illus. by Kate Seredy. **[CH 1945]**

Cinderella (Folk tale)—Adaptations
San Souci, Robert D. *The Talking Eggs: A Folktale from the American South.* Illus. by Jerry Pinkney. **[CH 1990]**

Steptoe, John. *Mufaro's Beautiful Daughters: An African Tale.* **[CH 1988]**

Circus—Fiction
Lathrop, Dorothy Pulis. *The Fairy Circus.* **[NH 1932]**

Schreiber, Georges. *Bambino the Clown.* **[CH 1948]**

Circus performers
Hunt, Mabel Leigh. *"Have You Seen Tom Thumb?"* **[NH 1943]**

Cities and towns in art
Johnson, Stephen T. *Alphabet City.* **[CH 1996]**

City and town life—China—Fiction
Lewis, Elizabeth Foreman. *Young Fu of the Upper Yangtze.* **[NA 1933]**

City and town life—Fiction
Burton, Virginia Lee. *The Little House.* **[CA 1943]**

Keats, Ezra Jack. *Goggles!* **[CH 1970]**

Sawyer, Ruth. *Roller Skates.* **[NA 1937]**

Shulevitz, Uri. *Snow.* **[CH 1999]**

Stewart, Sarah. *The Gardener.* Illus. by David Small. **[CH 1998]**

City and town life—Florida—Fiction

DiCamillo, Kate. *Because of Winn-Dixie.* [NH 2001]

City and town life—Poetry

McGinley, Phyllis. *All Around the Town.* Illus. by Helen Stone. [CH 1949]

Civil rights—Southern States—Fiction

Curtis, Christopher Paul. *The Watsons Go to Birmingham—1963.* [NH 1996]

Civil rights workers—India—Biography

Eaton, Jeanette. *Gandhi, Fighter without a Sword.* [NH 1951]

Civil rights workers—United States—Biography

Rappaport, Doreen. *Martin's Big Words: The Life of Dr. Martin Luther King, Jr.* Illus. by Bryan Collier. [CH 2002]

Civilization—History

Foster, Genevieve. *Birthdays of Freedom. Vol. 1. America's Heritage from the Ancient World.* [NH 1953]

Clergy—Biography

Rappaport, Doreen. *Martin's Big Words: The Life of Dr. Martin Luther King, Jr.* Illus. by Bryan Collier. [CH 2002]

Clergy—Fiction

Rylant, Cynthia. *A Fine White Dust.* [NH 1987]

Clipper ships—Fiction

Hewes, Agnes Danforth. *Glory of the Seas.* [NH 1934]

Meigs, Cornelia. *Clearing Weather.* [NH 1929]

Sperry, Armstrong. *All Sail Set: A Romance of the Flying Cloud.* [NH 1936]

Cloning—Fiction

Farmer, Nancy. *The House of the Scorpion.* [NH 2003]

Clothing and dress—Folklore

Taback, Simms. *Joseph Had a Little Overcoat.* [CA 2000]

Clouds—Fiction

Wiesner, David. *Sector 7.* [CH 2000]

Clowns—Fiction

Schreiber, Georges. *Bambino the Clown.* [CH 1948]

Coastal ecology

Goudey, Alice E. *Houses from the Sea.* Illus. by Adrienne Adams. [CH 1960]

Coastal ecology—Maine—Fiction

McCloskey, Robert. *Time of Wonder.* [CA 1958]

Coats—Folklore

Taback, Simms. *Joseph Had a Little Overcoat.* [CA 2000]

Color

Crews, Donald. *Freight Train.* [CH 1979]

Ehlert, Lois. *Color Zoo.* [CH 1990]

Young, Ed. *Seven Blind Mice.* [CH 1993]

Color—Fiction

Zolotow, Charlotte. *Mr. Rabbit and the Lovely Present.* Illus. by Maurice Sendak. [CH 1963]

Colorado—Fiction
Barnes, Nancy. *Wonderful Year.* [NH 1947]

Communication—Fiction
Raschka, Christopher. *Yo! Yes?* [CH 1994]

Connecticut—Fiction
Bianco, Margery Williams. *Winterbound.* [NH 1937]

Estes, Eleanor. *The Middle Moffat.* [NH 1943]

Estes, Eleanor. *Rufus M.* [NH 1944]

Lenski, Lois. *Phebe Fairchild, Her Book.* [NH 1937]

Connecticut—History—Fiction
Collier, James Lincoln & Christopher. *My Brother Sam Is Dead.* [NH 1975]

Constellations—Fiction
Maxwell, William. *The Heavenly Tenants.* [NH 1947]

Constitutional history—United States
Johnson, Gerald W. *America Is Born: A History for Peter.* [NH 1960]

Contests—Fiction
Konigsburg, E. L. *The View from Saturday.* [NA 1997]

Cookery—Fiction
Sawyer, Ruth. *The Christmas Anna Angel.* Illus. by Kate Seredy. [CH 1945]

Cookery—Pasta—Folklore
de Paola, Tomie. *Strega Nona: An Old Tale.* [CH 1976]

Cooks—Fiction
Brown, Marcia. *Skipper John's Cook.* [CH 1952]

Cooperativeness—Fiction
Ets, Marie Hall. *Mr. T. W. Anthony Woo.* [CH 1952]

Graham, Al. *Timothy Turtle.* Illus. by Tony Palazzo. [CH 1947]

Corn—Fiction
Buff, Mary & Conrad. *Magic Maize.* [NH 1954]

Rhoads, Dorothy. *The Corn Grows Ripe.* [NH 1957]

Costume—Fiction
du Bois, William Pène. *Bear Party.* [CH 1952]

Cotton picking—Fiction
Williams, Sherley Anne. *Working Cotton.* Illus. by Carole Byard. [CH 1993]

Counting
Feelings, Muriel. *Moja Means One: Swahili Counting Book.* Illus. by Tom Feelings. [CH 1972]

Moss, Lloyd. *Zin! Zin! Zin! A Violin.* Illus. by Marjorie Priceman. [CH 1996]

Tudor, Tasha. *1 Is One.* [CH 1957]

Young, Ed. *Seven Blind Mice.* [CH 1993]

Counting—Songs and music
Emberley, Barbara. *One Wide River to Cross.* Illus. by Ed Emberley. [CH 1967]

Counting-out rhymes
Bang, Molly. *Ten, Nine, Eight.* [CH 1984]

Country life—Canada—Fiction
Kingman, Lee. *Pierre Pidgeon.* Illus. by Arnold E. Bare. [CH 1944]

Country life—Illinois—Fiction
Peck, Richard. *A Long Way from Chicago.* [NH 1999]

Peck, Richard. *A Year Down Yonder.* [NA 2001]

Country life—Italy—Fiction
Angelo, Valenti. *Nino.* [NH 1939]

Country life—New Hampshire—Fiction
Bailey, Carolyn Sherwin. *Miss Hickory.* [NA 1947]

Country life—Pennsylvania—Fiction
Sorensen, Virginia. *Miracles on Maple Hill.* [NA 1957]

Country life—Wisconsin
North, Sterling. *Rascal: A Memoir of a Better Era.* [NH 1964]

Courage—Fiction
Armstrong, William H. *Sounder.* [NA 1970]

Dalgliesh, Alice. *The Courage of Sarah Noble.* [NH 1955]

Edmonds, Walter Dumaux. *The Matchlock Gun.* [NA 1942]

George, Jean Craighead. *Julie of the Wolves.* [NA 1973]

L'Engle, Madeleine. *A Wrinkle in Time.* [NA 1963]

Malkus, Alida. *The Dark Star of Itza.* [NH 1931]

O'Brien, Robert C. *Mrs. Frisby and the Rats of NIMH.* [NA 1972]

Sperry, Armstrong. *Call It Courage.* [NA 1941]

Spinelli, Jerry. *Wringer.* [NH 1998]

Stolz, Mary. *Belling the Tiger.* [NH 1962]

Treffinger, Carolyn. *Li Lun, Lad of Courage.* [NH 1948]

Wojciechowska, Maia. *Shadow of a Bull.* [NA 1965]

Courtship—Fiction
Langstaff, John. *Frog Went-A-Courtin'.* Illus. by Fedor Rojankovsky. [CA 1956]

Wilder, Laura Ingalls. *These Happy Golden Years.* [NH 1944]

Courtship—Folklore
Artzybasheff, Boris. *Seven Simeons: A Russian Tale.* [CH 1938]

Hogrogian, Nonny. *The Contest.* [CH 1977]

Cousins—Fiction
Enright, Elizabeth. *Gone-Away Lake.* [NH 1958]

Meigs, Cornelia. *The Windy Hill.* [NH 1922]

Seredy, Kate. *The Good Master.* [NH 1936]

Seredy, Kate. *The Singing Tree.* [NH 1940]

White, Ruth. *Belle Prater's Boy.* [NH 1997]

Cowboys—Legends
Bowman, James Cloyd. *Pecos Bill, the Greatest Cowboy of All Times.* [NH 1938]

Cows—Fiction
Bishop, Claire Huchet. *All Alone.* [NH 1954]

Cronin, Doreen. *Click, Clack, Moo: Cows That Type.* Illus. by Betsy Lewin. [CH 2001]

Leaf, Munro. *Wee Gillis*. Illus. by Robert Lawson. **[CH 1939]**

Macaulay, David. *Black and White*. **[CA 1991]**

Creation—Folklore

Hamilton, Virginia. *In the Beginning: Creation Stories from Around the World*. **[NH 1989]**

Crete (Greece)—Fiction

Berry, Erick. *The Winged Girl of Knossos*. **[NH 1934]**

Crickets—Fiction

Caudill, Rebecca. *A Pocketful of Cricket*. Illus. by Evaline Ness. **[CH 1965]**

Selden, George, pseud. (George Thompson). *The Cricket in Times Square*. **[NH 1961]**

Crime—Poetry

Zemach, Harve. *The Judge: An Untrue Tale*. Illus. by Margot Zemach. **[CH 1970]**

Crockett, Davy, 1786–1836

Rourke, Constance. *Davy Crockett*. **[NH 1935]**

Crossbows—Fiction

Marshall, Bernard G. *Cedric the Forester*. **[NH 1922]**

Crow Indians—Fiction

McGraw, Eloise Jarvis. *Moccasin Trail*. **[NH 1953]**

Crows—Fiction

Yashima, Taro. *Crow Boy*. **[CH 1956]**

Cuba—Fiction

Hawes, Charles. *The Great Quest*. **[NH 1922]**

Czech Republic—Folklore

Wisniewski, David. *Golem*. **[CA 1997]**

D

Dance—Fiction

Ackerman, Karen. *Song and Dance Man*. Illus. by Stephen Gammell. **[CA 1989]**

McKissack, Patricia C. *Mirandy and Brother Wind*. Illus. by Jerry Pinkney. **[CH 1989]**

de Paola, Tomie

de Paola, Tomie. *26 Fairmount Avenue*. **[NH 2000]**

Deaf—Fiction

Hubbard, Ralph. *Queer Person*. **[NH 1931]**

Death—Fiction

Blos, Joan W. *A Gathering of Days: A New England Girl's Journal, 1830–1832*. **[NA 1980]**

Collier, James Lincoln & Christopher. *My Brother Sam Is Dead*. **[NH 1975]**

Conly, Jane Leslie. *Crazy Lady*. **[NH 1994]**

Couloumbis, Audrey. *Getting Near to Baby*. **[NH 2000]**

Creech, Sharon. *Walk Two Moons*. **[NA 1995]**

L'Engle, Madeleine. *A Ring of Endless Light*. **[NH 1981]**

Mazer, Norma Fox. *After the Rain*. **[NH 1988]**

Miles, Miska. *Annie and the Old One*. **[NH 1972]**

Paterson, Katherine. *Bridge to Terabithia*. **[NA 1978]**

Rylant, Cynthia. *Missing May*. **[NA 1993]**

Subject Index to Newbery and Caldecott Books

Deception—Fiction
Elkin, Benjamin. *Gillespie and the Guards*. Illus. by James Daugherty. [CH 1957]

Deer—Fiction
Buff, Mary & Conrad. *Dash and Dart*. [CH 1943]

Leaf, Munro. *Wee Gillis*. Illus. by Robert Lawson. [CH 1939]

Denmark—Fiction
Lowry, Lois. *Number the Stars*. [NA 1990]

Dentists—Fiction
Steig, William. *Doctor De Soto*. [NH 1983]

Depression, Mental—Fiction
L'Engle, Madeleine. *A Ring of Endless Light*. [NH 1981]

Depressions—1929—Fiction
Curtis, Christopher Paul. *Bud, Not Buddy*. [NA 2000]

Hesse, Karen. *Out of the Dust*. [NA 1998]

Peck, Richard. *A Long Way from Chicago*. [NH 1999]

Peck, Richard. *A Year Down Yonder*. [NA 2001]

Taylor, Mildred D. *Roll of Thunder, Hear My Cry*. [NA 1977]

Desert ecology—West (U.S.)
Baylor, Byrd. *The Desert Is Theirs*. Illus. by Peter Parnall. [CH 1976]

Deserts—Fiction
Staples, Suzanne Fisher. *Shabanu, Daughter of the Wind*. [NH 1990]

Deserts—West (U.S.)
Baylor, Byrd. *The Desert Is Theirs*. Illus. by Peter Parnall. [CH 1976]

Devil—Folklore
Zemach, Harve. *Duffy and the Devil: A Cornish Tale*. Illus. by Margot Zemach. [CA 1974]

Diaries—Fiction
Blos, Joan W. *A Gathering of Days: A New England Girl's Journal, 1830–1832*. [NA 1980]

Cushman, Karen. *Catherine, Called Birdy*. [NH 1995]

Diners (Restaurants)—Fiction
Bauer, Joan. *Hope Was Here*. [NH 2001]

Dinosaurs—Fiction
Rohmann, Eric. *Time Flies*. [CH 1995]

Dinosaurs—Models—History—19th century
Kerley, Barbara. *The Dinosaurs of Waterhouse Hawkins: An Illuminating History of Mr. Waterhouse Hawkins, Artist and Lecturer*. Illus. by Brian Selznick. [CH 2002]

Discipline of children—Fiction
Shannon, David. *No, David!* [CH 1999]

Discrimination—Fiction
Conly, Jane Leslie. *Crazy Lady*. [NH 1994]

Field, Rachel. *Calico Bush*. [NH 1932]

Hader, Berta & Elmer. *Cock-a-Doodle Doo*. [CH 1940]

Handforth, Thomas. *Mei Li*. [CA 1939]

Krumgold, Joseph. *Onion John.* [NA 1960]

Divorce—Fiction

Cleary, Beverly. *Dear Mr. Henshaw.* [NA 1984]

Paulsen, Gary. *Hatchet.* [NH 1988]

Voigt, Cynthia. *A Solitary Blue.* [NH 1984]

Dogs—Fiction

Armstrong, William H. *Sounder.* [NA 1970]

Bemelmans, Ludwig. *Madeline's Rescue.* [CA 1954]

DeJong, Meindert. *Along Came a Dog.* [NH 1959]

DeJong, Meindert. *Hurry Home, Candy.* [NH 1954]

DiCamillo, Kate. *Because of Winn-Dixie.* [NH 2001]

Estes, Eleanor. *Ginger Pye.* [NA 1952]

Gág, Wanda. *Nothing At All.* [CH 1942]

Gipson, Fred. *Old Yeller.* [NH 1957]

Gray, Elizabeth Janet (Elizabeth Gray Vining). *Adam of the Road.* [NA 1943]

McCarty, Peter. *Hondo & Fabian.* [CH 2003]

Naylor, Phyllis Reynolds. *Shiloh.* [NA 1992]

Newberry, Clare Turlay. *Barkis.* [CH 1939]

Rankin, Louise. *Daughter of the Mountains.* [NH 1949]

Rathmann, Peggy. *Officer Buckle and Gloria.* [CA 1996]

Simont, Marc. *The Stray Dog.* [CH 2002]

Van Allsburg, Chris. *The Garden of Abdul Gasazi.* [CH 1980]

Will, pseud. (William Lipkind). *Finders Keepers.* Illus. by Nicolas, pseud. (Nicolas Mordvinoff). [CA 1952]

Yorinks, Arthur. *Hey, Al.* Illus. by Richard Egielski. [CA 1987]

Dogsledding—Fiction

Paulsen, Gary. *Dogsong.* [NH 1986]

Dolittle, Doctor (Fictitious character)

Lofting, Hugh. *The Voyages of Doctor Dolittle.* [NA 1923]

Dolls—Fiction

Bailey, Carolyn Sherwin. *Miss Hickory.* [NA 1947]

Field, Rachel. *Hitty, Her First Hundred Years.* [NA 1930]

McGinley, Phyllis. *The Most Wonderful Doll in the World.* Illus. by Helen Stone. [CH 1951]

Parrish, Anne. *Floating Island.* [NH 1931]

Dolphins—Fiction

L'Engle, Madeleine. *A Ring of Endless Light.* [NH 1981]

Donkeys—Fiction

Steig, William. *Sylvester and the Magic Pebble.* [CA 1970]

Dragons—Fiction

Gannett, Ruth S. *My Father's Dragon.* [NH 1949]

Dragons—Folklore

Hodges, Margaret. *Saint George and the Dragon.* Illus. by Trina Schart Hyman. [CA 1985]

Dreams—Fiction

Parrish, Anne. *The Dream Coach.* [NH 1925]

Ringgold, Faith. *Tar Beach.* [CH 1992]

Wiesner, David. *Free Fall.* **[CH 1989]**

Dreams—Folklore

Shulevitz, Uri. *The Treasure.* **[CH 1980]**

Druids and druidism—Fiction

Pope, Elizabeth Marie. *The Perilous Gard.* **[NH 1975]**

Ducks—Fiction

Davis, Lavinia R. *The Wild Birthday Cake.* Illus. by Hildegard Woodward. **[CH 1950]**

McCloskey, Robert. *Make Way for Ducklings.* **[CA 1942]**

Tafuri, Nancy. *Have You Seen My Duckling?* **[CH 1985]**

Dumplings—Folklore

Mosel, Arlene. *The Funny Little Woman.* Illus. by Blair Lent. **[CA 1973]**

Dust storms—Fiction

Hesse, Karen. *Out of the Dust.* **[NA 1998]**

Dutch Americans—Fiction

Moore, Annie Carroll. *Nicholas: A Manhattan Christmas Story.* **[NH 1925]**

Dwarfs—Biography

Hunt, Mabel Leigh. *"Have You Seen Tom Thumb?"* **[NH 1943]**

Dwarfs—Folklore

Gág, Wanda. *Snow White and the Seven Dwarfs.* Adapted from the Brothers Grimm. **[CH 1939]**

Jarrell, Randall. *Snow-White and the Seven Dwarfs.* Illus. by Nancy Ekholm Burkert; adapted from the Brothers Grimm. **[CH 1973]**

E

Earthquakes—California—Fiction

Yep, Laurence. *Dragonwings.* **[NH 1976]**

Easter—Fiction

Milhous, Katherine. *The Egg Tree.* **[CA 1951]**

Politi, Leo. *Juanita.* **[CH 1949]**

Eccentrics and eccentricities—Fiction

Krumgold, Joseph. *Onion John.* **[NA 1960]**

Raskin, Ellen. *Figgs & Phantoms.* **[NH 1975]**

Tolan, Stephanie S. *Surviving the Applewhites.* **[NH 2003]**

Ecology—West (U.S.)

Baylor, Byrd. *The Desert Is Theirs.* Illus. by Peter Parnall. **[CH 1976]**

Egg decoration—Fiction

Milhous, Katherine. *The Egg Tree.* **[CA 1951]**

Egypt—History—To 332 B.C.—Fiction

McGraw, Eloise Jarvis. *The Golden Goblet.* **[NH 1962]**

Elephants—Folklore

Young, Ed. *Seven Blind Mice.* **[CH 1993]**

Ellington, Duke, 1899–1974

Pinkney, Andrea Davis. *Duke Ellington: The Piano Prince and the Orchestra.* Illus. by Brian Pinkney. **[CH 1999]**

Elves—Fiction
Lisle, Janet Taylor. *Afternoon of the Elves*. [NH 1990]

Empire State Building (New York, N.Y.)—Fiction
Wiesner, David. *Sector 7*. [CH 2000]

England—Fiction
Cooper, Susan. *The Dark Is Rising*. [NH 1974]

Henry, Marguerite. *King of the Wind*. [NA 1949]

Pope, Elizabeth Marie. *The Perilous Gard*. [NH 1975]

England—Folklore
Brown, Marcia. *Dick Whittington and His Cat*. [CH 1951]

Hodges, Margaret. *Saint George and the Dragon*. Illus. by Trina Schart Hyman. [CA 1985]

Ness, Evaline. *Tom Tit Tot: An English Folk Tale*. [CH 1966]

Shulevitz, Uri. *The Treasure*. [CH 1980]

Zemach, Harve. *Duffy and the Devil: A Cornish Tale*. Illus. by Margot Zemach. [CA 1974]

England—Legends
Malcolmson, Anne, editor. *Song of Robin Hood*. Illus. by Virginia Lee Burton. [CH 1948]

England—Social life and customs—1066-1485—Fiction
Cushman, Karen. *Catherine, Called Birdy*. [NH 1995]

Cushman, Karen. *The Midwife's Apprentice*. [NA 1996]

England—Songs and music
Malcolmson, Anne, editor. *Song of Robin Hood*. Illus. by Virginia Lee Burton. [CH 1948]

Entertainers—Fiction
Ackerman, Karen. *Song and Dance Man*. Illus. by Stephen Gammell. [CA 1989]

Environmental protection—Fiction
Hiaasen, Carl. *Hoot*. [NH 2003]

Envy—Fiction
Lionni, Leo. *Alexander and the Wind-Up Mouse*. [CH 1970]

Escapes—Fiction
Keats, Ezra Jack. *Goggles!* [CH 1970]

Eskimos—Ethnic identity—Fiction
George, Jean Craighead. *Julie of the Wolves*. [NA 1973]

Paulsen, Gary. *Dogsong*. [NH 1986]

Eskimos—Fiction
Lide, Alice Alison. *Ood-le-uk the Wanderer*. [NH 1931]

Ethnicity—Peru—Fiction
Clark, Ann Nolan. *Secret of the Andes*. [NA 1953]

Ethnology—Africa
Musgrove, Margaret. *Ashanti to Zulu: African Traditions*. Illus. by Leo & Diane Dillon. [CA 1977]

Etiquette—Fiction
Joslin, Sesyle. *What Do You Say, Dear?* Illus. by Maurice Sendak. [CH 1959]

Low, Joseph. *Mice Twice*. [CH 1981]

Europe, Eastern—Folklore
Taback, Simms. *Joseph Had a Little Overcoat*. [CA 2000]

Europe—History—18th century
Gurko, Leo. *Tom Paine, Freedom's Apostle.* [NH 1958]

Explorers—Fiction
O'Dell, Scott. *The King's Fifth.* [NH 1967]

Explorers—Latin America
Shippen, Katherine. *New Found World.* [NH 1946]

Explorers—Norway—Biography
Hall, Anna Gertrude. *Nansen.* [NH 1941]

F

Fables
Brown, Marcia. *Once a Mouse.* [CA 1962]

Cooney, Barbara. *Chanticleer and the Fox.* Text adapted from *Canterbury Tales.* [CA 1959]

Daugherty, James. *Andy and the Lion.* [CH 1939]

Lobel, Arnold. *Fables.* [CA 1981]

Young, Ed. *Seven Blind Mice.* [CH 1993]

Fairies—Fiction
Lathrop, Dorothy Pulis. *The Fairy Circus.* [NH 1932]

McGraw, Eloise Jarvis. *Moorchild.* [NH 1997]

Fairs—Fiction
Ets, Marie Hall. *Mr. Penny's Race Horse.* [CH 1957]

Fairy tales
Andersen, H. C. (Hans Christian). *The Steadfast Tin Soldier.* Illus. by Marcia Brown; trans. by M. R. James. [CH 1954]

Brown, Marcia. *Cinderella, or the Little Glass Slipper.* Adapted from Charles Perrault. [CA 1955]

Brown, Marcia. *Puss in Boots.* Adapted from Charles Perrault. [CH 1953]

Gág, Wanda. *Snow White and the Seven Dwarfs.* [CH 1939]

Hyman, Trina Schart. *Little Red Riding Hood.* [CH 1984]

Jarrell, Randall. *Snow-White and the Seven Dwarfs.* Illus. by Nancy Ekholm Burkert; adapted from the Brothers Grimm. [CH 1973]

Lesser, Rika. *Hansel and Gretel.* Illus. by Paul O. Zelinsky. [CH 1985]

Marcellino, Fred. *Puss in Boots.* Trans. by Malcolm Arthur; adapted from Charles Perrault. [CH 1991]

Ness, Evaline. *Tom Tit Tot: An English Folk Tale.* [CH 1966]

Pinkney, Jerry. *The Ugly Duckling.* Adapted from Hans Christian Andersen. [CH 2000]

Plume, Ilse. *The Bremen-Town Musicians.* Adapted from the Brothers Grimm. [CH 1981]

Young, Ella. *The Wonder Smith and His Son.* [NH 1928]

Zelinsky, Paul O. *Rapunzel.* [CA 1998]

Zelinsky, Paul O. *Rumpelstiltskin.* [CH 1987]

Fairy tales—Adaptations
Marshall, James. *Goldilocks and the Three Bears.* [CH 1989]

San Souci, Robert D. *The Talking Eggs: A Folktale from the American South.* Illus. by Jerry Pinkney. [CH 1990]

Scieszka, Jon. *The Stinky Cheese Man and Other Fairly Stupid Tales.* Illus. by Lane Smith. **[CH 1993]**

Steptoe, John. *Mufaro's Beautiful Daughters: An African Tale.* **[CH 1988]**

Wiesner, David. *The Three Pigs.* **[CA 2002]**

Young, Ed. *Lon Po Po: A Red-Riding Hood Story from China.* **[CA 1990]**

Family—History

Clark, Ann Nolan. *Secret of the Andes.* **[NA 1953]**

Lawson, Robert. *They Were Strong and Good.* **[CA 1941]**

Family life—Chesapeake Bay Region (Md. and Va.)—Fiction

Voigt, Cynthia. *Dicey's Song.* **[NA 1983]**

Family life—Colorado—Fiction

Barnes, Nancy. *Wonderful Year.* **[NH 1947]**

Family life—Connecticut—Fiction

Estes, Eleanor. *The Middle Moffat.* **[NH 1943]**

Estes, Eleanor. *Rufus M.* **[NH 1944]**

Lenski, Lois. *Phebe Fairchild, Her Book.* **[NH 1937]**

Family life—Denmark—Fiction

Lowry, Lois. *Number the Stars.* **[NA 1990]**

Family life—England—Fiction

Cushman, Karen. *Catherine, Called Birdy.* **[NH 1995]**

Family life—Fiction

Caudill, Rebecca. *Tree of Freedom.* **[NH 1950]**

Creech, Sharon. *Walk Two Moons.* **[NA 1995]**

Creech, Sharon. *The Wanderer.* **[NH 2001]**

Curtis, Christopher Paul. *The Watsons Go to Birmingham—1963.* **[NH 1996]**

Dalgliesh, Alice. *The Courage of Sarah Noble.* **[NH 1955]**

Estes, Eleanor. *Ginger Pye.* **[NA 1952]**

Giff, Patricia Reilly. *Pictures of Hollis Woods.* **[NH 2003]**

Hunt, Irene. *Up a Road Slowly.* **[NA 1967]**

Lenski, Lois. *Strawberry Girl.* **[NA 1946]**

Lindquist, Jennie. *The Golden Name Day.* **[NH 1956]**

Lowry, Lois. *The Giver.* **[NA 1994]**

MacLachlan, Patricia. *Sarah, Plain and Tall.* **[NA 1986]**

Martin, Ann M. *A Corner of the Universe.* **[NH 2003]**

Mathis, Sharon Bell. *The Hundred Penny Box.* **[NH 1976]**

McCloskey, Robert. *One Morning in Maine.* **[CH 1953]**

McGraw, Eloise Jarvis. *Moccasin Trail.* **[NH 1953]**

Stolz, Mary. *The Noonday Friends.* **[NH 1966]**

Williams, Sherley Anne. *Working Cotton.* Illus. by Carole Byard. **[CH 1993]**

Williams, Vera B. *A Chair for My Mother.* **[CH 1983]**

Williams, Vera B. *"More More More," Said the Baby: Three Love Stories.* **[CH 1991]**

Zion, Gene. *All Falling Down.* Illus. by Margaret Bloy Graham. **[CH 1952]**

Subject Index to Newbery and Caldecott Books 27

Family life—Italy—Fiction
Angelo, Valenti. *Nino.* [NH 1939]

Family life—Minnesota—Fiction
Wilder, Laura Ingalls. *On the Banks of Plum Creek.* [NH 1938]

Family life—New York (State)—Fiction
Edmonds, Walter Dumaux. *The Matchlock Gun.* [NA 1942]

Family life—North Carolina—Fiction
Tolan, Stephanie S. *Surviving the Applewhites.* [NH 2003]

Family life—Ohio River—Fiction
Crawford, Phyllis. *"Hello, the Boat!"* [NH 1939]

Family life—Oregon—Fiction
Cleary, Beverly. *Ramona Quimby, Age 8.* [NH 1982]

Family life—San Joaquin Valley (Calif.)—Fiction
Gates, Doris. *Blue Willow.* [NH 1941]

Family life—South Dakota—Fiction
Wilder, Laura Ingalls. *By the Shores of Silver Lake.* [NH 1940]

Wilder, Laura Ingalls. *Little Town on the Prairie.* [NH 1942]

Wilder, Laura Ingalls. *The Long Winter.* [NH 1941]

Wilder, Laura Ingalls. *These Happy Golden Years.* [NH 1944]

Family life—Texas—Fiction
Gipson, Fred. *Old Yeller.* [NH 1957]

Family life—Wales—Fiction
Bond, Nancy. *A String in the Harp.* [NH 1977]

Family life—West Virginia—Fiction
Rylant, Cynthia. *Missing May.* [NA 1993]

Rylant, Cynthia. *The Relatives Came.* Illus. by Stephen Gammell. [CH 1986]

Rylant, Cynthia. *When I Was Young in the Mountains.* Illus. by Diane Goode. [CH 1983]

Family problems—Fiction
Armstrong, William H. *Sounder.* [NA 1970]

Coman, Carolyn. *What Jamie Saw.* [NH 1996]

Hamilton, Virginia. *Sweet Whispers, Brother Rush.* [NH 1983]

Ish-Kishor, Sulamith. *Our Eddie.* [NH 1970]

Lisle, Janet Taylor. *Afternoon of the Elves.* [NH 1990]

Neville, Emily. *It's Like This, Cat.* [NA 1964]

Paterson, Katherine. *Jacob Have I Loved.* [NA 1981]

Raskin, Ellen. *Figgs & Phantoms.* [NH 1975]

Snyder, Zilpha Keatley. *The Headless Cupid.* [NH 1972]

Sorensen, Virginia. *Miracles on Maple Hill.* [NA 1957]

Voigt, Cynthia. *A Solitary Blue.* [NH 1984]

Family problems—Harlem (New York, N.Y.)—Fiction
Myers, Walter Dean. *Scorpions.* [NH 1989]

Family problems—Mississippi—Fiction
Taylor, Mildred D. *Roll of Thunder, Hear My Cry.* [NA 1977]

Family problems—Ohio—Fiction

Hamilton, Virginia. *M. C. Higgins, the Great.* [NA 1975]

Fantasy fiction

Alexander, Lloyd. *The Black Cauldron.* [NH 1966]

Alexander, Lloyd. *The High King.* [NA 1969]

Bailey, Carolyn Sherwin. *Miss Hickory.* [NA 1947]

Berry, Erick. *The Winged Girl of Knossos.* [NH 1934]

Besterman, Catherine. *The Quaint and Curious Quest of Johnny Longfoot.* [NH 1948]

Bond, Nancy. *A String in the Harp.* [NH 1977]

Cooper, Susan. *The Dark Is Rising.* [NH 1974]

Cooper, Susan. *The Grey King.* [NA 1976]

du Bois, William Pène. *The Twenty-One Balloons.* [NA 1948]

Engdahl, Sylvia Louise. *Enchantress from the Stars.* [NH 1971]

Field, Rachel. *Hitty, Her First Hundred Years.* [NA 1930]

Gannett, Ruth S. *My Father's Dragon.* [NH 1949]

Jarrell, Randall. *The Animal Family.* [NH 1966]

Kendall, Carol. *The Gammage Cup.* [NH 1960]

Krauss, Ruth. *A Very Special House.* Illus. by Maurice Sendak. [CH 1954]

Langton, Jane. *The Fledgling.* [NH 1981]

Lathrop, Dorothy Pulis. *The Fairy Circus.* [NH 1932]

Lawson, Robert. *Rabbit Hill.* [NA 1945]

Le Guin, Ursula K. *The Tombs of Atuan.* [NH 1972]

Levine, Gail Carson. *Ella Enchanted.* [NH 1998]

Lofting, Hugh. *The Voyages of Doctor Dolittle.* [NA 1923]

Maxwell, William. *The Heavenly Tenants.* [NH 1947]

McGraw, Eloise Jarvis. *Moorchild.* [NH 1997]

McKinley, Robin. *The Blue Sword.* [NH 1983]

McKinley, Robin. *The Hero and the Crown.* [NA 1985]

Moore, Annie Carroll. *Nicholas: A Manhattan Christmas Story.* [NH 1925]

O'Brien, Robert C. *Mrs. Frisby and the Rats of NIMH.* [NA 1972]

Parrish, Anne. *The Dream Coach.* [NH 1925]

Pope, Elizabeth Marie. *The Perilous Gard.* [NH 1975]

Rawlings, Marjorie Kinnan. *The Secret River.* [NH 1956]

Sauer, Julia. *Fog Magic.* [NH 1944]

Selden, George, pseud. (George Thompson). *The Cricket in Times Square.* [NH 1961]

Sendak, Maurice. *In the Night Kitchen.* [CH 1971]

Sendak, Maurice. *Outside Over There.* [CH 1982]

Sendak, Maurice. *Where the Wild Things Are.* [CA 1964]

Seuss, Dr., pseud. (Theodor Seuss Geisel). *Bartholomew and the Oobleck.* [CH 1950]

Seuss, Dr., pseud. (Theodor Seuss Geisel). *If I Ran the Zoo.* [CH 1951]

Seuss, Dr., pseud. (Theodor Seuss Geisel). *McElligot's Pool.* [CH 1948]

Singer, Isaac Bashevis. *The Fearsome Inn.* [NH 1968]

Steele, Mary Q. *Journey Outside.* [NH 1970]

Steig, William. *Abel's Island.* [NH 1977]

Stolz, Mary. *Belling the Tiger.* [NH 1962]

Turner, Megan Whalen. *The Thief.* [NH 1997]

Van Allsburg, Chris. *Jumanji.* [CA 1982]

White, E. B. *Charlotte's Web.* [NH 1952]

Wiesner, David. *Free Fall.* [CH 1989]

Wiesner, David. *Tuesday.* [CA 1992]

Fantasy games—Fiction

Snyder, Zilpha Keatley. *The Egypt Game.* [NH 1968]

Farm life—Bulgaria—Fiction

Shannon, Monica. *Dobry.* [NA 1935]

Farm life—Connecticut—Fiction

Bianco, Margery Williams. *Winterbound.* [NH 1937]

Farm life—Fiction

Blos, Joan W. *A Gathering of Days: A New England Girl's Journal, 1830–1832.* [NA 1980]

Caudill, Rebecca. *A Pocketful of Cricket.* Illus. by Evaline Ness. [CH 1965]

Hall, Donald. *Ox-Cart Man.* Illus. by Barbara Cooney. [CA 1980]

Preston, Edna Mitchell. *Pop Corn & Ma Goodness.* Illus. by Robert Andrew Parker. [CH 1970]

White, E. B. *Charlotte's Web.* [NH 1952]

Yates, Elizabeth. *Mountain Born.* [NH 1944]

Farm life—Hungary—Fiction

Seredy, Kate. *The Good Master.* [NH 1936]

Seredy, Kate. *The Singing Tree.* [NH 1940]

Farm life—Illinois—Fiction

Hunt, Irene. *Across Five Aprils.* [NH 1965]

Farm life—Minnesota—Fiction

Paulsen, Gary. *The Winter Room.* [NH 1990]

Farm life—Oklahoma—Fiction

Hesse, Karen. *Out of the Dust.* [NA 1998]

Farm life—Pennsylvania—Fiction

de Angeli, Marguerite. *Yonie Wondernose.* [CH 1945]

Farm life—Scotland—Fiction

Leaf, Munro. *Wee Gillis.* Illus. by Robert Lawson. [CH 1939]

Farm life—Wisconsin—Fiction

Enright, Elizabeth. *Thimble Summer.* [NA 1939]

Fathers and daughters—Fiction

Bang, Molly. *Ten, Nine, Eight.* [CH 1984]

Berry, Erick. *The Winged Girl of Knossos.* [NH 1934]

Cleary, Beverly. *Ramona and Her Father.* [NH 1978]

Dalgliesh, Alice. *The Courage of Sarah Noble.* [NH 1955]

Malkus, Alida. *The Dark Star of Itza.* [NH 1931]

Snedeker, Caroline Dale. *The Forgotten Daughter.* [NH 1934]

Yolen, Jane. *Owl Moon.* Illus. by John Schoenherr. [CA 1988]

Fathers and daughters—Folklore

Yolen, Jane. *The Emperor and the Kite.* Illus. by Ed Young. [CH 1968]

Fathers and sons—Fiction

Bartone, Elisa. *Peppe the Lamplighter.* Illus. by Ted Lewin. [CH 1994]

Best, Herbert. *Garram the Hunter: A Boy of the Hill Tribes.* [NH 1931]

Buff, Mary & Conrad. *The Apple and the Arrow.* [NH 1952]

Collier, James Lincoln & Christopher. *My Brother Sam Is Dead.* [NH 1975]

Gantos, Jack. *Joey Pigza Loses Control.* [NH 2001]

Ish-Kishor, Sulamith. *Our Eddie.* [NH 1970]

Jukes, Mavis. *Like Jake and Me.* [NH 1985]

Kelly, Eric P. *The Trumpeter of Krakow.* [NA 1929]

Krumgold, Joseph. *Onion John.* [NA 1960]

Kyle, Anne. *The Apprentice of Florence.* [NH 1934]

Myers, Walter Dean. *Somewhere in the Darkness.* [NH 1993]

Neville, Emily. *It's Like This, Cat.* [NA 1964]

Paterson, Katherine. *Bridge to Terabithia.* [NA 1978]

Voigt, Cynthia. *A Solitary Blue.* [NH 1984]

Yep, Laurence. *Dragonwings.* [NH 1976]

Fathers and sons—Legends

McDermott, Gerald. *Arrow to the Sun: A Pueblo Indian Tale.* [CA 1975]

Fear—Fiction

Henkes, Kevin. *Owen.* [CH 1994]

McCully, Emily Arnold. *Mirette on the High Wire.* [CA 1993]

Wojciechowska, Maia. *Shadow of a Bull.* [NA 1965]

Feathers—Fiction

Olds, Elizabeth. *Feather Mountain.* [CH 1952]

Ferris wheels—Fiction

Lawson, Robert. *The Great Wheel.* [NH 1958]

Finland—History—Fiction

Davis, Julia. *Vaino: A Boy of New Finland.* [NH 1930]

Finn MacCool (Legendary character)

Young, Ella. *The Tangle-Coated Horse and Other Tales.* [NH 1930]

Finnish Americans—Fiction

Holm, Jennifer L. *Our Only May Amelia.* [NH 2000]

Stong, Phil. *Honk, the Moose.* [NH 1936]

Fires—Illinois—Chicago—History—19th century

Murphy, Jim. *The Great Fire.* [NH 1996]

First ladies—United States—Biography

Freedman, Russell. *Eleanor Roosevelt: A Life of Discovery.* [NH 1994]

Fishers—Virgin Islands—Fiction
Brown, Marcia. *Henry Fisherman.* [CH 1950]

Fishes—Fiction
Lionni, Leo. *Swimmy.* [CH 1964]

Fishes—Poetry
Seuss, Dr., pseud. (Theodor Seuss Geisel). *McElligot's Pool.* [CH 1948]

Fishing—Fiction
Goffstein, M. B. *Fish for Supper.* [CH 1977]

Fishing boats—Fiction
Brown, Marcia. *Skipper John's Cook.* [CH 1952]

Flies—Poetry
Howitt, Mary. *The Spider and the Fly.* Illus. by Tony DiTerlizzi. [CH 2003]

Flight—Fiction
Baylor, Byrd. *Hawk, I'm Your Brother.* Illus. by Peter Parnall. [CH 1977]

Langton, Jane. *The Fledgling.* [NH 1981]

Ringgold, Faith. *Tar Beach.* [CH 1992]

Florida—Fiction
DiCamillo, Kate. *Because of Winn-Dixie.* [NH 2001]

Hiaasen, Carl. *Hoot.* [NH 2003]

Lenski, Lois. *Strawberry Girl.* [NA 1946]

Rawlings, Marjorie Kinnan. *The Secret River.* [NH 1956]

Flying Cloud (Clipper-ship)—Fiction
Hewes, Agnes Danforth. *Glory of the Seas.* [NH 1934]

Sperry, Armstrong. *All Sail Set: A Romance of the Flying Cloud.* [NH 1936]

Fog—Fiction
Sauer, Julia. *Fog Magic.* [NH 1944]

Tresselt, Alvin. *Hide and Seek Fog.* Illus. by Roger Duvoisin. [CH 1966]

Folk songs—England
Malcolmson, Anne, editor. *Song of Robin Hood.* Illus. by Virginia Lee Burton. [CH 1948]

Folk songs—Scotland
Leodhas, Sorche Nic, pseud. (Leclaire Alger). *Always Room for One More.* Illus. by Nonny Hogrogian. [CA 1966]

Folk songs—United States
Emberley, Barbara. *One Wide River to Cross.* Illus. by Ed Emberley. [CH 1967]

Langstaff, John. *Frog Went-A-Courtin'.* Illus. by Fedor Rojankovsky. [CA 1956]

Spier, Peter. *Fox Went Out on a Chilly Night: An Old Song.* [CH 1962]

Taback, Simms. *There Was an Old Lady Who Swallowed a Fly.* [CH 1998]

Folklore
Hamilton, Virginia. *In the Beginning: Creation Stories from Around the World.* [NH 1989]

Folklore—Africa
Courlander, Harold. *The Cow-Tail Switch, and Other West African Stories.* [NH 1948]

Dayrell, Elphinstone. *Why the Sun and the Moon Live in the Sky: A Nigerian Tale.* Illus. by Blair Lent. **[CH 1969]**

Grifalconi, Ann. *The Village of Round and Square Houses.* **[CH 1987]**

Haley, Gail E. *A Story A Story: An African Tale.* **[CA 1971]**

McDermott, Gerald. *Anansi the Spider: A Tale from the Ashanti.* **[CH 1973]**

Steptoe, John. *Mufaro's Beautiful Daughters: An African Tale.* **[CH 1988]**

Folklore—Africa, West

Aardema, Verna. *Why Mosquitoes Buzz in People's Ears: A West African Tale.* Illus. by Leo & Diane Dillon. **[CA 1976]**

Folklore—Alaska

Sleator, William. *The Angry Moon.* Illus. by Blair Lent. **[CH 1971]**

Folklore—Armenia

Hogrogian, Nonny. *The Contest.* **[CH 1977]**

Hogrogian, Nonny. *One Fine Day.* **[CA 1972]**

Folklore—Cameroon

Grifalconi, Ann. *The Village of Round and Square Houses.* **[CH 1987]**

Folklore—China

Chan, Chih-Yi. *Good-Luck Horse.* Illus. by Plato Chan. **[CH 1944]**

Yolen, Jane. *The Emperor and the Kite.* Illus. by Ed Young. **[CH 1968]**

Young, Ed. *Lon Po Po: A Red-Riding Hood Story from China.* **[CA 1990]**

Folklore—Cornwall (England : County)

Zemach, Harve. *Duffy and the Devil: A Cornish Tale.* Illus. by Margot Zemach. **[CA 1974]**

Folklore—Czech Republic

Wisniewski, David. *Golem.* **[CA 1997]**

Folklore—England

Brown, Marcia. *Dick Whittington and His Cat.* **[CH 1951]**

Hodges, Margaret. *Saint George and the Dragon.* Illus. by Trina Schart Hyman. **[CA 1985]**

Ness, Evaline. *Tom Tit Tot: An English Folk Tale.* **[CH 1966]**

Shulevitz, Uri. *The Treasure.* **[CH 1980]**

Zemach, Harve. *Duffy and the Devil: A Cornish Tale.* Illus. by Margot Zemach. **[CA 1974]**

Folklore—Europe, Eastern

Taback, Simms. *Joseph Had a Little Overcoat.* **[CA 2000]**

Folklore—France

Brown, Marcia. *Cinderella, or the Little Glass Slipper.* Adapted from Charles Perrault. **[CA 1955]**

Brown, Marcia. *Puss in Boots.* Adapted from Charles Perrault. **[CH 1953]**

Brown, Marcia. *Stone Soup.* **[CH 1948]**

Marcellino, Fred. *Puss in Boots.* Trans. by Malcolm Arthur; adapted from Charles Perrault. **[CH 1991]**

Folklore—Germany

Gág, Wanda. *Snow White and the Seven Dwarfs.* **[CH 1939]**

Hyman, Trina Schart. *Little Red Riding Hood.* [CH 1984]

Jarrell, Randall. *Snow-White and the Seven Dwarfs.* Illus. by Nancy Ekholm Burkert; adapted from the Brothers Grimm. [CH 1973]

Lesser, Rika. *Hansel and Gretel.* Illus. by Paul O. Zelinsky. [CH 1985]

Plume, Ilse. *The Bremen-Town Musicians.* Adapted from the Brothers Grimm. [CH 1981]

Zelinsky, Paul O. *Rapunzel.* [CA 1998]

Zelinsky, Paul O. *Rumpelstiltskin.* [CH 1987]

Folklore—Hungary

Seredy, Kate. *The White Stag.* [NA 1938]

Folklore—India

Brown, Marcia. *Once a Mouse.* [CA 1962]

Young, Ed. *Seven Blind Mice.* [CH 1993]

Folklore—Ireland

Colum, Padraic. *The Big Tree of Bunlahy, Stories of My Own Countryside.* [NH 1934]

Young, Ella. *The Tangle-Coated Horse and Other Tales.* [NH 1930]

Young, Ella. *The Wonder Smith and His Son.* [NH 1928]

Folklore—Italy

Davis, Mary Gould. *The Truce of the Wolf and Other Tales of Old Italy.* [NH 1932]

de Paola, Tomie. *Strega Nona: An Old Tale.* [CH 1976]

Folklore—Japan

Hodges, Margaret. *The Wave.* Illus. by Blair Lent. [CH 1965]

Mosel, Arlene. *The Funny Little Woman.* Illus. by Blair Lent. [CA 1973]

Snyder, Diane. *The Boy of the Three-Year Nap.* Illus. by Allen Say. [CH 1989]

Folklore—Martinique

San Souci, Robert D. *The Faithful Friend.* Illus. by Brian Pinkney. [CH 1996]

Folklore—Nigeria

Dayrell, Elphinstone. *Why the Sun and the Moon Live in the Sky: A Nigerian Tale.* Illus. by Blair Lent. [CH 1969]

Folklore—Northwest, Pacific

McDermott, Gerald. *Raven: A Trickster Tale from the Pacific Northwest.* [CH 1994]

Folklore—Poland

Singer, Isaac Bashevis. *When Shlemiel Went to Warsaw and Other Stories.* [NH 1969]

Singer, Isaac Bashevis. *Zlateh the Goat and Other Stories.* [NH 1967]

Folklore—Prague (Czech Republic)

Wisniewski, David. *Golem.* [CA 1997]

Folklore—Russia

Artzybasheff, Boris. *Seven Simeons: A Russian Tale.* [CH 1938]

Ransome, Arthur. *The Fool of the World and the Flying Ship.* Illus. by Uri Shulevitz. [CA 1969]

Reyher, Becky. *My Mother is the Most Beautiful Woman in the World.* Illus. by Ruth Chrisman Gannett. [CH 1946]

Robbins, Ruth. *Baboushka and the Three Kings.* Illus. by Nicolas Sidjakov. [CA 1961]

Folklore—Scotland

Leodhas, Sorche Nic, pseud. (Leclaire Alger). *All in the Morning Early.* Illus. by Evaline Ness. [CH 1964]

Leodhas, Sorche Nic, pseud. (Leclaire Alger). *Thistle and Thyme: Tales and Legends from Scotland.* [NH 1963]

Young, Ella. *The Tangle-Coated Horse and Other Tales.* [NH 1930]

Folklore—South America

Finger, Charles. *Tales from Silver Lands.* [NA 1925]

Folklore—Southern States

San Souci, Robert D. *The Talking Eggs: A Folktale from the American South.* Illus. by Jerry Pinkney. [CH 1990]

Folklore—Ukraine

Reyher, Becky. *My Mother is the Most Beautiful Woman in the World.* Illus. by Ruth Chrisman Gannett. [CH 1946]

Folklore—United States

Lester, Julius. *John Henry.* Illus. by Jerry Pinkney. [CH 1995]

Sawyer, Ruth. *Journey Cake, Ho!* Illus. by Robert McCloskey. [CH 1954]

Stevens, Janet. *Tops & Bottoms.* [CH 1996]

Folklore—West Indies

San Souci, Robert D. *The Faithful Friend.* Illus. by Brian Pinkney. [CH 1996]

Forest animals—Fiction

Ets, Marie Hall. *In the Forest.* [CH 1945]

Krauss, Ruth. *The Happy Day.* Illus. by Marc Simont. [CH 1950]

Forests and forestry—Fiction

Ets, Marie Hall. *In the Forest.* [CH 1945]

Marshall, Bernard G. *Cedric the Forester.* [NH 1922]

Fort Vancouver (Wash.)—Fiction

Carr, Mary Jane. *Young Mac of Fort Vancouver.* [NH 1941]

Fortification

Macaulay, David. *Castle.* [CH 1978]

Fortune, Amos, 1709 or 10-1801

Yates, Elizabeth. *Amos Fortune, Free Man.* [NA 1951]

Foster home care—Fiction

Curtis, Christopher Paul. *Bud, Not Buddy.* [NA 2000]

Giff, Patricia Reilly. *Pictures of Hollis Woods.* [NH 2003]

Horvath, Polly. *Everything on a Waffle.* [NH 2002]

Paterson, Katherine. *The Great Gilly Hopkins.* [NH 1979]

Foxes—Fiction

Cooney, Barbara. *Chanticleer and the Fox.* Text adapted from *Canterbury Tales.* [CA 1959]

Davis, Lavinia R. *Roger and the Fox.* Illus. by Hildegard Woodward. [CH 1948]

Spier, Peter. *Fox Went Out on a Chilly Night: An Old Song.* [CH 1962]

Steig, William. *The Amazing Bone.* [CH 1977]

Steig, William. *Doctor De Soto.* [NH 1983]

Foxes—Folklore

Hogrogian, Nonny. *One Fine Day.* [CA 1972]

France—Fiction

Bishop, Claire Huchet. *All Alone.* [NH 1954]

Fisher, Cyrus, pseud. (Darwin L. Teilhet). *The Avion My Uncle Flew.* [NH 1947]

France—Folklore

Brown, Marcia. *Cinderella, or the Little Glass Slipper.* Adapted from Charles Perrault. [CA 1955]

Brown, Marcia. *Puss in Boots.* Adapted from Charles Perrault. [CH 1953]

Brown, Marcia. *Stone Soup.* [CH 1948]

Marcellino, Fred. *Puss in Boots.* Trans. by Malcolm Arthur; adapted from Charles Perrault. [CH 1991]

France—History—Revolution, 1789–1799

Eaton, Jeanette. *A Daughter of the Seine: The Life of Madame Roland.* [NH 1930]

Gurko, Leo. *Tom Paine, Freedom's Apostle.* [NH 1958]

France—History—20th century

Provensen, Alice & Martin. *The Glorious Flight: Across the Channel with Louis Bleriot.* [CA 1984]

Freedom

Foster, Genevieve. *Birthdays of Freedom. Vol. 1. America's Heritage from the Ancient World.* [NH 1953]

Freedom—Fiction

Avi. *Nothing but the Truth: A Documentary Novel.* [NH 1992]

Freedom of religion—Fiction

Gaggin, Eva Roe. *Down Ryton Water.* [NH 1942]

Freedom of religion—History

Eaton, Jeanette. *Lone Journey: The Life of Roger Williams.* [NH 1945]

French language—Readers

Frasconi, Antonio. *The House That Jack Built: La Maison Que Jacques A Batie.* [CH 1959]

Freshwater animals—Fiction

Fleming, Denise. *In the Small, Small Pond.* [CH 1994]

Friendship—Fiction

Barnes, Nancy. *Wonderful Year.* [NH 1947]

Bauer, Marion Dane. *On My Honor.* [NH 1987]

Bishop, Claire Huchet. *All Alone.* [NH 1954]

Bishop, Claire Huchet. *Pancakes-Paris.* [NH 1948]

Brooks, Bruce. *The Moves Make the Man.* [NH 1985]

Conly, Jane Leslie. *Crazy Lady.* [NH 1994]

Creech, Sharon. *Walk Two Moons.* [NA 1995]

de Regniers, Beatrice Schenk. *May I Bring a Friend?* Illus. by Beni Montresor. [CA 1965]

Estes, Eleanor. *The Hundred Dresses.* [NH 1945]

Giff, Patricia Reilly. *Lily's Crossing.* [NH 1998]

Greene, Bette. *Philip Hall Likes Me, I Reckon Maybe.* [NH 1975]

Hamilton, Virginia. *The Planet of Junior Brown.* [NH 1972]

Konigsburg, E. L. *Jennifer, Hecate, Macbeth, William McKinley, and Me, Elizabeth.* [NH 1968]

Konigsburg, E. L. *The View from Saturday.* [NA 1997]

Krumgold, Joseph. *Onion John.* [NA 1960]

Lisle, Janet Taylor. *Afternoon of the Elves.* [NH 1990]

Lobel, Arnold. *Frog and Toad Are Friends.* [CH 1971]

Lobel, Arnold. *Frog and Toad Together.* [NH 1973]

Lowry, Lois. *Number the Stars.* [NA 1990]

Martin, Ann M. *A Corner of the Universe.* [NH 2003]

Neville, Emily. *It's Like This, Cat.* [NA 1964]

Newberry, Clare Turlay. *Marshmallow.* [CH 1943]

Paterson, Katherine. *Bridge to Terabithia.* [NA 1978]

Paterson, Katherine. *Jacob Have I Loved.* [NA 1981]

Raschka, Christopher. *Yo! Yes?* [CH 1994]

Rohmann, Eric. *My Friend Rabbit.* [CA 2003]

Rylant, Cynthia. *A Fine White Dust.* [NH 1987]

Sachar, Louis. *Holes.* [NA 1999]

Sawyer, Ruth. *Roller Skates.* [NA 1937]

Selden, George, pseud. (George Thompson). *The Cricket in Times Square.* [NH 1961]

Snedeker, Caroline Dale. *Downright Dencey.* [NH 1928]

Snyder, Zilpha Keatley. *The Egypt Game.* [NH 1968]

Speare, Elizabeth George. *The Bronze Bow.* [NA 1962]

Speare, Elizabeth George. *The Sign of the Beaver.* [NH 1984]

Stolz, Mary. *The Noonday Friends.* [NH 1966]

White, E. B. *Charlotte's Web.* [NH 1952]

Friendship—Folklore

San Souci, Robert D. *The Faithful Friend.* Illus. by Brian Pinkney. [CH 1996]

Friendship—Songs and music

Leodhas, Sorche Nic, pseud. (Leclaire Alger). *Always Room for One More.* Illus. by Nonny Hogrogian. [CA 1966]

Fritz, Jean—Fiction

Fritz, Jean and Margot Tomes. *Homesick: My Own Story.* [NH 1983]

Frogs—Fiction

Lobel, Arnold. *Frog and Toad Are Friends.* [CH 1971]

Lobel, Arnold. *Frog and Toad Together.* [NH 1973]

Wiesner, David. *Tuesday.* [CA 1992]

Frontier and pioneer life

Tunis, Edwin. *Frontier Living.* [NH 1962]

Frontier and pioneer life—Connecticut—Fiction

Dalgliesh, Alice. *The Courage of Sarah Noble.* [NH 1955]

Frontier and pioneer life—Fiction

Hunt, Mabel Leigh. *Better Known as Johnny Appleseed.* [NH 1951]

MacLachlan, Patricia. *Sarah, Plain and Tall.* [NA 1986]

Meader, Stephen W. *Boy with a Pack.* [NH 1940]

Meigs, Cornelia. *Swift Rivers*. [NH 1933]

Frontier and pioneer life—Kentucky—Fiction

Caudill, Rebecca. *Tree of Freedom*. [NH 1950]

Frontier and pioneer life—Maine—Fiction

Field, Rachel. *Calico Bush*. [NH 1932]

Speare, Elizabeth George. *The Sign of the Beaver*. [NH 1984]

Frontier and pioneer life—Minnesota—Fiction

Wilder, Laura Ingalls. *On the Banks of Plum Creek*. [NH 1938]

Frontier and pioneer life—New York (State)—Fiction

Edmonds, Walter Dumaux. *The Matchlock Gun*. [NA 1942]

Frontier and pioneer life—South Dakota—Fiction

McNeely, Marian Hurd. *The Jumping-Off Place*. [NH 1930]

Wilder, Laura Ingalls. *By the Shores of Silver Lake*. [NH 1940]

Wilder, Laura Ingalls. *Little Town on the Prairie*. [NH 1942]

Wilder, Laura Ingalls. *The Long Winter*. [NH 1941]

Wilder, Laura Ingalls. *These Happy Golden Years*. [NH 1944]

Frontier and pioneer life—Tennessee—Fiction

Issacs, Anne. *Swamp Angel*. Illus. by Paul O. Zelinsky. [CH 1995]

Frontier and pioneer life—Texas—Fiction

Gipson, Fred. *Old Yeller*. [NH 1957]

Frontier and pioneer life—Washington (State)—Fiction

Holm, Jennifer L. *Our Only May Amelia*. [NH 2000]

Frontier and pioneer life—West (U.S.)—Fiction

McGraw, Eloise Jarvis. *Moccasin Trail*. [NH 1953]

Frontier and pioneer life—Wisconsin—Fiction

Brink, Carol Ryrie. *Caddie Woodlawn*. [NA 1936]

Havighurst, Walter & Marion. *Song of the Pines: A Story of Norwegian Lumbering in Wisconsin*. [NH 1950]

Frontier and pioneer life—Wyoming—Fiction

Schmidt, Sarah. *New Land, a Novel for Boys and Girls*. [NH 1934]

Fugitive slaves—Fiction

Blos, Joan W. *A Gathering of Days: A New England Girl's Journal, 1830–1832*. [NA 1980]

Swift, Hildegarde Hoyt. *The Railroad to Freedom: A Story of the Civil War*. [NH 1933]

Fur traders—Fiction

Carr, Mary Jane. *Young Mac of Fort Vancouver*. [NH 1941]

Future life—Fiction

Farmer, Nancy. *The Ear, the Eye, and the Arm*. [NH 1995]

Farmer, Nancy. *The House of the Scorpion*. [NH 2003]

Lowry, Lois. *The Giver*. [NA 1994]

G

Galileo, 1564–1642

Sís, Peter. *Starry Messenger: A Book Depicting the Life of a Famous*

Scientist, Mathematician, Astronomer, Philosopher, Physicist, Galileo Galilei. [CH 1997]

Games—Fiction
Van Allsburg, Chris. *Jumanji.* [CA 1982]

Gandhi, Mahatma, 1869-1948
Eaton, Jeanette. *Gandhi, Fighter without a Sword.* [NH 1951]

Gangs—Fiction
Myers, Walter Dean. *Scorpions.* [NH 1989]

Gardening—Fiction
Stewart, Sarah. *The Gardener.* Illus. by David Small. [CH 1998]

Gardens—Boston (Mass.)—Fiction
McCloskey, Robert. *Make Way for Ducklings.* [CA 1942]

Gaspé Peninsula (Québec)—Fiction
Kingman, Lee. *Pierre Pidgeon.* Illus. by Arnold E. Bare. [CH 1944]

Genealogy
Lawson, Robert. *They Were Strong and Good.* [CA 1941]

Generals—United States—Biography
Foster, Genevieve. *George Washington.* [NH 1950]

Foster, Genevieve. *George Washington's World.* [NH 1942]

Genius—Fiction
Fenner, Carol. *Yolonda's Genius.* [NH 1996]

Geographical myths
Colum, Padraic. *The Voyagers: Being Legends and Romances of Atlantic Discovery.* [NH 1926]

George, Saint, d. 303—Folklore
Hodges, Margaret. *Saint George and the Dragon.* Illus. by Trina Schart Hyman. [CA 1985]

Germany—Folklore
Gág, Wanda. *Snow White and the Seven Dwarfs.* [CH 1939]

Hyman, Trina Schart. *Little Red Riding Hood.* [CH 1984]

Jarrell, Randall. *Snow-White and the Seven Dwarfs.* Illus. by Nancy Ekholm Burkert; adapted from the Brothers Grimm. [CH 1973]

Lesser, Rika. *Hansel and Gretel.* Illus. by Paul O. Zelinsky. [CH 1985]

Plume, Ilse. *The Bremen-Town Musicians.* Adapted from the Brothers Grimm. [CH 1981]

Zelinsky, Paul O. *Rapunzel.* [CA 1998]

Zelinsky, Paul O. *Rumpelstiltskin.* [CH 1987]

Ghosts—Fiction
Hamilton, Virginia. *Sweet Whispers, Brother Rush.* [NH 1983]

McKissack, Patricia. *The Dark-Thirty: Southern Tales of the Supernatural.* [NH 1993]

Giant sequoia—Fiction
Buff, Mary & Conrad. *Big Tree.* [NH 1947]

Gifted children—Fiction
L'Engle, Madeleine. *A Wrinkle in Time.* [NA 1963]

Paterson, Katherine. *Bridge to Terabithia.* [NA 1978]

Gifts—Fiction

Van Allsburg, Chris. *The Polar Express.* [CA 1986]

Zolotow, Charlotte. *Mr. Rabbit and the Lovely Present.* Illus. by Maurice Sendak. [CH 1963]

Goblins—Fiction

Kimmel, Eric. *Hershel and the Hanukkah Goblins.* Illus. by Trina Schart Hyman. [CH 1990]

Sendak, Maurice. *Outside Over There.* [CH 1982]

Gold—Fiction

O'Dell, Scott. *The King's Fifth.* [NH 1967]

Golden Fleece (Greek mythology)

Colum, Padraic. *The Golden Fleece and the Heroes Who Lived before Achilles.* [NH 1922]

Golem

McDermott, Beverly Brodsky. *The Golem: A Jewish Legend.* [CH 1977]

Wisniewski, David. *Golem.* [CA 1997]

Grail—Fiction

Jewett, Eleanore. *The Hidden Treasure of Glaston.* [NH 1947]

Grand Canyon (Ariz.)—Discovery and exploration—Fiction

O'Dell, Scott. *The King's Fifth.* [NH 1967]

Grandfathers—Fiction

Ackerman, Karen. *Song and Dance Man.* Illus. by Stephen Gammell. [CA 1989]

Creech, Sharon. *The Wanderer.* [NH 2001]

L'Engle, Madeleine. *A Ring of Endless Light.* [NH 1981]

Mazer, Norma Fox. *After the Rain.* [NH 1988]

Say, Allen. *Grandfather's Journey.* [CA 1994]

Grandmothers—Fiction

Goffstein, M. B. *Fish for Supper.* [CH 1977]

Miles, Miska. *Annie and the Old One.* [NH 1972]

Paterson, Katherine. *Jacob Have I Loved.* [NA 1981]

Peck, Richard. *A Long Way from Chicago.* [NH 1999]

Peck, Richard. *A Year Down Yonder.* [NA 2001]

Voigt, Cynthia. *Dicey's Song.* [NA 1983]

Williams, Vera B. *A Chair for My Mother.* [CH 1983]

Grandparents—Fiction

Creech, Sharon. *Walk Two Moons.* [NA 1995]

Minarik, Else H. *Little Bear's Visit.* Illus. by Maurice Sendak. [CH 1962]

Gravity—Fiction

Zion, Gene. *All Falling Down.* Illus. by Margaret Bloy Graham. [CH 1952]

Great Britain—History—Edward III, 1327–1377—Fiction

Avi. *Crispin: The Cross of Lead.* [NA 2003]

Great Britain—History—Henry II, 1154–1189—Fiction

Jewett, Eleanore. *The Hidden Treasure of Glaston.* [NH 1947]

Great Britain—History—Medieval period, 1066–1485—Fiction

de Angeli, Marguerite. *The Door in the Wall.* [NA 1950]

Gray, Elizabeth Janet (Elizabeth Gray Vining). *Adam of the Road.* [NA 1943]

Great Fire, Chicago, Ill., 1871

Murphy, Jim. *The Great Fire.* [NH 1996]

Great Lakes—Fiction

Holling, Holling C. *Paddle-to-the-Sea.* [CH 1942]

Great-aunts—Fiction

Mathis, Sharon Bell. *The Hundred Penny Box.* [NH 1976]

Greece—Biography

Coolidge, Olivia. *Men of Athens.* [NH 1963]

Greece—History—Athenian supremacy, 479–431 B.C.

Coolidge, Olivia. *Men of Athens.* [NH 1963]

Greed—Fiction

O'Dell, Scott. *The King's Fifth.* [NH 1967]

Gregorian chants

Ford, Lauren. *The Ageless Story.* [CH 1940]

Grief—Fiction

Couloumbis, Audrey. *Getting Near to Baby.* [NH 2000]

Paterson, Katherine. *Bridge to Terabithia.* [NA 1978]

Rylant, Cynthia. *Missing May.* [NA 1993]

Growth—Fiction

Clark, Ann Nolan. *Secret of the Andes.* [NA 1953]

Dalgliesh, Alice. *The Silver Pencil.* [NH 1945]

de Angeli, Marguerite. *The Door in the Wall.* [NA 1950]

de Angeli, Marguerite. *Yonie Wondernose.* [CH 1945]

Gipson, Fred. *Old Yeller.* [NH 1957]

Hunt, Irene. *Up a Road Slowly.* [NA 1967]

Krumgold, Joseph. *... And Now Miguel.* [NA 1954]

McGraw, Eloise Jarvis. *The Golden Goblet.* [NH 1962]

Rhoads, Dorothy. *The Corn Grows Ripe.* [NH 1957]

Schaefer, Jack. *Old Ramon.* [NH 1961]

Ullman, James Ramsey. *Banner in the Sky.* [NH 1955]

Guards troops—Fiction

Elkin, Benjamin. *Gillespie and the Guards.* Illus. by James Daugherty. [CH 1957]

Guatemala—Fiction

Buff, Mary & Conrad. *Magic Maize.* [NH 1954]

Gubbaun Saor (Irish mythology)

Young, Ella. *The Wonder Smith and His Son.* [NH 1928]

Guilt—Fiction

Bauer, Marion Dane. *On My Honor.* [NH 1987]

Fox, Paula. *One-Eyed Cat.* [NH 1985]

Guinea, Gulf of—Fiction
Hawes, Charles. *The Great Quest.* [NH 1922]

Gulls—Fiction
Holling, Holling C. *Seabird.* [NH 1949]

Turkle, Brinton. *Thy Friend, Obadiah.* [CH 1970]

Gypsies—Fiction
Jones, Idwal. *Whistler's Van.* [NH 1937]

H

Handicapped—Fiction
de Angeli, Marguerite. *The Door in the Wall.* [NA 1950]

Gray, Elizabeth Janet (Elizabeth Gray Vining). *Young Walter Scott.* [NH 1936]

Hubbard, Ralph. *Queer Person.* [NH 1931]

Jewett, Eleanore. *The Hidden Treasure of Glaston.* [NH 1947]

Konigsburg, E. L. *The View from Saturday.* [NA 1997]

Hanukkah—Fiction
Kimmel, Eric. *Hershel and the Hanukkah Goblins.* Illus. by Trina Schart Hyman. [CH 1990]

Hares—Folklore
Stevens, Janet. *Tops & Bottoms.* [CH 1996]

Harlem (New York, N.Y.)—Fiction
Myers, Walter Dean. *Scorpions.* [NH 1989]

Ringgold, Faith. *Tar Beach.* [CH 1992]

Weik, Mary Hays. *The Jazz Man.* [NH 1967]

Harlem (New York, N.Y.)—Poetry
Myers, Walter Dean. *Harlem.* Illus. by Christopher Myers. [CH 1998]

Hawkins, B. Waterhouse (Benjamin Waterhouse), 1807–1889
Kerley, Barbara. *The Dinosaurs of Waterhouse Hawkins: An Illuminating History of Mr. Waterhouse Hawkins, Artist and Lecturer.* Illus. by Brian Selznick. [CH 2002]

Hawks—Fiction
Baylor, Byrd. *Hawk, I'm Your Brother.* Illus. by Peter Parnall. [CH 1977]

Henry the Navigator, 1394–1460—Fiction
Colum, Padriac. *The Voyagers: Being Legends and Romances of Atlantic Discovery.* [NH 1926]

Henry V, King of England, 1387–1422—Fiction
Whitney, Elinor. *Tod of the Fens.* [NH 1929]

Hispanic Americans—Fiction
Krumgold, Joseph. *... And Now Miguel.* [NA 1954]

Hispanic Americans—Social life and customs—Fiction
Politi, Leo. *Juanita.* [CH 1949]

Politi, Leo. *Pedro, the Angel of Olvera Street.* [CH 1947]

Historical fiction
Armstrong, William H. *Sounder.* [NA 1970]

Avi. *Crispin: The Cross of Lead.* **[NA 2003]**

Blos, Joan W. *A Gathering of Days: A New England Girl's Journal, 1830–1832.* **[NA 1980]**

Brink, Carol Ryrie. *Caddie Woodlawn.* **[NA 1936]**

Carr, Mary Jane. *Young Mac of Fort Vancouver.* **[NH 1941]**

Caudill, Rebecca. *Tree of Freedom.* **[NH 1950]**

Collier, James Lincoln & Christopher. *My Brother Sam Is Dead.* **[NH 1975]**

Colum, Padraic. *The Voyagers: Being Legends and Romances of Atlantic Discovery.* **[NH 1926]**

Curtis, Christopher Paul. *Bud, Not Buddy.* **[NA 2000]**

Curtis, Christopher Paul. *The Watsons Go to Birmingham—1963.* **[NH 1996]**

Cushman, Karen. *Catherine, Called Birdy.* **[NH 1995]**

Cushman, Karen. *The Midwife's Apprentice.* **[NA 1996]**

Dalgliesh, Alice. *The Courage of Sarah Noble.* **[NH 1955]**

Dalgliesh, Alice. *The Thanksgiving Story.* Illus. by Helen Sewell. **[CH 1955]**

Davis, Julia. *Mountains Are Free.* **[NH 1931]**

Davis, Julia. *Vaino: A Boy of New Finland.* **[NH 1930]**

de Angeli, Marguerite. *Black Fox of Lorne.* **[NH 1957]**

de Angeli, Marguerite. *The Door in the Wall.* **[NA 1950]**

DeJong, Meindert. *The House of Sixty Fathers.* **[NH 1957]**

Edmonds, Walter Dumaux. *The Matchlock Gun.* **[NA 1942]**

Field, Rachel. *Calico Bush.* **[NH 1932]**

Forbes, Esther. *Johnny Tremain.* **[NA 1944]**

Fox, Paula. *The Slave Dancer.* **[NA 1974]**

Gaggin, Eva Roe. *Down Ryton Water.* **[NH 1942]**

Giff, Patricia Reilly. *Lily's Crossing.* **[NH 1998]**

Gipson, Fred. *Old Yeller.* **[NH 1957]**

Gray, Elizabeth Janet (Elizabeth Gray Vining). *Adam of the Road.* **[NA 1943]**

Gray, Elizabeth Janet (Elizabeth Gray Vining). *Meggy MacIntosh.* **[NH 1931]**

Gray, Elizabeth Janet (Elizabeth Gray Vining). *Young Walter Scott.* **[NH 1936]**

Hallock, Grace. *The Boy Who Was.* **[NH 1929]**

Havighurst, Walter & Marion. *Song of the Pines: A Story of Norwegian Lumbering in Wisconsin.* **[NH 1950]**

Hesse, Karen. *Out of the Dust.* **[NA 1998]**

Hewes, Agnes Danforth. *The Codfish Musket.* **[NH 1937]**

Hewes, Agnes Danforth. *Spice and the Devil's Cave.* **[NH 1931]**

Holm, Jennifer L. *Our Only May Amelia.* **[NH 2000]**

Hunt, Irene. *Across Five Aprils.* **[NH 1965]**

Hunt, Mabel Leigh. *Better Known as Johnny Appleseed.* **[NH 1951]**

Jewett, Eleanore. *The Hidden Treasure of Glaston.* **[NH 1947]**

Keith, Harold. *Rifles for Watie.* **[NA 1958]**

Kelly, Eric P. *The Trumpeter of Krakow.* **[NA 1929]**

Kyle, Anne. *The Apprentice of Florence.* [NH 1934]

Latham, Jean Lee. *Carry On, Mr. Bowditch.* [NA 1956]

Lawson, Robert. *The Great Wheel.* [NH 1958]

Lenski, Lois. *Indian Captive: the Story of Mary Jemison.* [NH 1942]

Lownsbery, Eloise. *Out of the Flame.* [NH 1932]

Lowry, Lois. *Number the Stars.* [NA 1990]

MacLachlan, Patricia. *Sarah, Plain and Tall.* [NA 1986]

Malkus, Alida. *The Dark Star of Itza.* [NH 1931]

McGraw, Eloise Jarvis. *The Golden Goblet.* [NH 1962]

McGraw, Eloise Jarvis. *Moccasin Trail.* [NH 1953]

McNeely, Marian Hurd. *The Jumping-Off Place.* [NH 1930]

Meader, Stephen W. *Boy with a Pack.* [NH 1940]

Means, Florence Crannell. *The Moved-Outers.* [NH 1946]

Meigs, Cornelia. *Clearing Weather.* [NH 1929]

Meigs, Cornelia. *Swift Rivers.* [NH 1933]

Miller, Elizabeth. *Pran of Albania.* [NH 1930]

Moon, Grace. *The Runaway Papoose.* [NH 1929]

Mukerji, Dhan Gopal. *Gay Neck, the Story of a Pigeon.* [NA 1928]

O'Dell, Scott. *The King's Fifth.* [NH 1967]

O'Dell, Scott. *Sing Down the Moon.* [NH 1971]

Park, Linda Sue. *A Single Shard.* [NA 2002]

Peck, Richard. *A Long Way from Chicago.* [NH 1999]

Peck, Richard. *A Year Down Yonder.* [NA 2001]

Schmidt, Sarah. *New Land, a Novel for Boys and Girls.* [NH 1934]

Seredy, Kate. *The Singing Tree.* [NH 1940]

Singmaster, Elsie. *Swords of Steel: The Story of a Gettysburg Boy.* [NH 1934]

Snedeker, Caroline Dale. *Downright Dencey.* [NH 1928]

Snedeker, Caroline Dale. *The Forgotten Daughter.* [NH 1934]

Speare, Elizabeth George. *The Bronze Bow.* [NA 1962]

Speare, Elizabeth George. *The Sign of the Beaver.* [NH 1984]

Speare, Elizabeth George. *The Witch of Blackbird Pond.* [NA 1959]

Steele, William O. *The Perilous Road.* [NH 1959]

Stong, Phil. *Honk, the Moose.* [NH 1936]

Swift, Hildegarde Hoyt. *Little Blacknose.* [NH 1930]

Swift, Hildegarde Hoyt. *The Railroad to Freedom: A Story of the Civil War.* [NH 1933]

Taylor, Mildred D. *Roll of Thunder, Hear My Cry.* [NA 1977]

Trevino, Elizabeth Borton de. *I, Juan de Pareja.* [NA 1966]

Whitney, Elinor. *Tod of the Fens.* [NH 1929]

Wilder, Laura Ingalls. *By the Shores of Silver Lake.* [NH 1940]

Wilder, Laura Ingalls. *Little Town on the Prairie.* [NH 1942]

Wilder, Laura Ingalls. *The Long Winter.* [NH 1941]

Wilder, Laura Ingalls. *On the Banks of Plum Creek.* [NH 1938]

Wilder, Laura Ingalls. *These Happy Golden Years.* [NH 1944]

Yep, Laurence. *Dragon's Gate.* [NH 1994]

Yep, Laurence. *Dragonwings.* [NH 1976]

History, Modern—18th century
Foster, Genevieve. *George Washington's World.* [NH 1942]

History, Modern—19th century
Foster, Genevieve. *Abraham Lincoln's World.* [NH 1945]

Holmes, Oliver Wendell, 1841–1935
Judson, Clara Ingram. *Mr. Justice Holmes.* [NH 1957]

Holocaust, Jewish (1939–1945)—Hungary
Siegal, Aranka. *Upon the Head of the Goat: A Childhood in Hungary, 1939–1944.* [NH 1982]

Holocaust, Jewish (1939–1945)—Netherlands
Reiss, Johanna. *The Upstairs Room.* [NH 1973]

Home—Fiction
Clark, Ann Nolan. *Secret of the Andes.* [NA 1953]

Homeless persons—Fiction
Carlson, Natalie Savage. *The Family under the Bridge.* [NH 1959]

Cushman, Karen. *The Midwife's Apprentice.* [NA 1996]

Hamilton, Virginia. *The Planet of Junior Brown.* [NH 1972]

Sachar, Louis. *Holes.* [NA 1999]

Spinelli, Jerry. *Maniac Magee.* [NA 1991]

Homesickness—Fiction
Say, Allen. *Grandfather's Journey.* [CA 1994]

Honesty—Fiction
Bauer, Marion Dane. *On My Honor.* [NH 1987]

Ness, Evaline. *Sam, Bangs & Moonshine.* [CA 1967]

Honesty—Poetry
Zemach, Harve. *The Judge: An Untrue Tale.* Illus. by Margot Zemach. [CH 1970]

Horror stories
McKissack, Patricia. *The Dark-Thirty: Southern Tales of the Supernatural.* [NH 1993]

Horse breeds—Fiction
Henry, Marguerite. *Justin Morgan Had a Horse.* [NH 1946]

Horses—Fiction
Henry, Marguerite. *Justin Morgan Had a Horse.* [NH 1946]

Henry, Marguerite. *King of the Wind.* [NA 1949]

James, Will. *Smoky, the Cowhorse.* [NA 1927]

Jones, Idwal. *Whistler's Van.* [NH 1937]

Sandoz, Mari. *The Horsecatcher.* [NH 1958]

Horses—Folklore
Chan, Chih-Yi. *Good-Luck Horse.* Illus. by Plato Chan. [CH 1944]

Goble, Paul. *The Girl Who Loved Wild Horses.* [CA 1979]

Hotels, motels, etc.—Fiction
Bemelmans, Ludwig. *The Golden Basket.* [NH 1937]

Hotels, motels, etc.—Poetry

Willard, Nancy. *A Visit to William Blake's Inn: Poems for Innocent and Experienced Travelers.* Illus. by Alice & Martin Provensen. [NA 1982, CH 1982]

Houses—Fiction

Burton, Virginia Lee. *The Little House.* [CA 1943]

Krauss, Ruth. *A Very Special House.* Illus. by Maurice Sendak. [CH 1954]

Human cloning—Fiction

Farmer, Nancy. *The House of the Scorpion.* [NH 2003]

Human relations—Fiction

Bunting, Eve. *Smoky Night.* Illus. by David Diaz. [CA 1995]

Human-animal communication—Fiction

Lofting, Hugh. *The Voyages of Doctor Dolittle.* [NA 1923]

Yashima, Taro. *Crow Boy.* [CH 1956]

Human-animal relationships

North, Sterling. *Rascal: A Memoir of a Better Era.* [NH 1964]

Human-animal relationships—Fiction

Daugherty, James. *Andy and the Lion.* [CH 1939]

Eckert, Allan W. *Incident at Hawk's Hill.* [NH 1972]

Ets, Marie Hall. *Play with Me.* [CH 1956]

Gág, Wanda. *Millions of Cats.* [NH 1929]

George, Jean Craighead. *Julie of the Wolves.* [NA 1973]

Gipson, Fred. *Old Yeller.* [NH 1957]

Henry, Marguerite. *King of the Wind.* [NA 1949]

James, Will. *Smoky, the Cowhorse.* [NA 1927]

Jarrell, Randall. *The Animal Family.* [NH 1966]

Langton, Jane. *The Fledgling.* [NH 1981]

Lawson, Robert. *Rabbit Hill.* [NA 1945]

O'Dell, Scott. *Island of the Blue Dolphins.* [NA 1961]

Pilkey, Dav. *The Paperboy.* [CH 1997]

Rathmann, Peggy. *Officer Buckle and Gloria.* [CA 1996]

Selden, George, pseud. (George Thompson). *The Cricket in Times Square.* [NH 1961]

Stong, Phil. *Honk, the Moose.* [NH 1936]

Turkle, Brinton. *Thy Friend, Obadiah.* [CH 1970]

Ward, Lynd. *The Biggest Bear.* [CA 1953]

Yates, Elizabeth. *Mountain Born.* [NH 1944]

Yorinks, Arthur. *Hey, Al.* Illus. by Richard Egielski. [CA 1987]

Human-animal relationships—Folklore

Goble, Paul. *The Girl Who Loved Wild Horses.* [CA 1979]

Human-animal relationships—Legends

Bowman, James Cloyd. *Pecos Bill, the Greatest Cowboy of All Times.* [NH 1938]

Humorous fiction

Atwater, Richard. *Mr. Popper's Penguins.* [NH 1939]

Bennett, John. *The Pigtail of Ah Lee Ben Loo.* [NH 1929]

Cleary, Beverly. *Ramona Quimby, Age 8.* [NH 1982]

Parrish, Anne. *The Story of Appleby Capple.* [NH 1951]

Whitney, Elinor. *Tod of the Fens.* [NH 1929]

Humorous poetry

Fish, Helen Dean. *Four and Twenty Blackbirds.* Illus. by Robert Lawson. [CH 1938]

Petersham, Maude & Miska. *The Rooster Crows: A Book of American Rhymes and Jingles.* [CA 1946]

Humorous stories

Davis, Mary Gould. *The Truce of the Wolf and Other Tales of Old Italy.* [NH 1932]

Joslin, Sesyle. *What Do You Say, Dear?* Illus. by Maurice Sendak. [CH 1959]

Lobel, Arnold. *Frog and Toad Are Friends.* [CH 1971]

Lobel, Arnold. *Frog and Toad Together.* [NH 1973]

Scieszka, Jon. *The Stinky Cheese Man and Other Fairly Stupid Tales.* Illus. by Lane Smith. [CH 1993]

Singer, Isaac Bashevis. *When Shlemiel Went to Warsaw and Other Stories.* [NH 1969]

Singer, Isaac Bashevis. *Zlateh the Goat and Other Stories.* [NH 1967]

Hungary—Fiction

Brown, Margaret Wise. *Wheel on the Chimney.* Illus. by Tibor Gergely. [CH 1955]

Sawyer, Ruth. *The Christmas Anna Angel.* Illus. by Kate Seredy. [CH 1945]

Seredy, Kate. *The Good Master.* [NH 1936]

Seredy, Kate. *The Singing Tree.* [NH 1940]

Hungary—Folklore

Seredy, Kate. *The White Stag.* [NA 1938]

Hunters—Fiction

Hader, Berta & Elmer. *The Mighty Hunter.* [CH 1944]

Jarrell, Randall. *The Animal Family.* [NH 1966]

Ward, Lynd. *The Biggest Bear.* [CA 1953]

Hymns

Wheeler, Opal. *Sing in Praise: A Collection of the Best Loved Hymns.* Illus. by Marjorie Torrey. [CH 1947]

I

Ice skating—Fiction

Van Stockum, Hilda. *A Day on Skates: The Story of a Dutch Picnic.* [NH 1935]

Idaho—Fiction

Creech, Sharon. *Walk Two Moons.* [NA 1995]

Identity—Fiction

Avi. *Crispin: The Cross of Lead.* [NA 2003]

McGraw, Eloise Jarvis. *Moccasin Trail.* [NH 1953]

McGraw, Eloise Jarvis. *Moorchild.* [NH 1997]

Paterson, Katherine. *Jacob Have I Loved.* [NA 1981]

Paulsen, Gary. *Dogsong.* [NH 1986]

Pinkney, Jerry. *The Ugly Duckling.* Adapted from Hans Christian Andersen. [CH 2000]

White, Ruth. *Belle Prater's Boy.* [NH 1997]

Illinois—Fiction

Hunt, Irene. *Across Five Aprils.* [NH 1965]

Peck, Richard. *A Long Way from Chicago.* [NH 1999]

Peck, Richard. *A Year Down Yonder.* [NA 2001]

Illustrators—Biography

de Paola, Tomie. *26 Fairmount Avenue.* [NH 2000]

Peet, Bill. *Bill Peet: An Autobiography.* [CH 1990]

Imaginary places—Fiction

Enright, Elizabeth. *Gone-Away Lake.* [NH 1958]

Kendall, Carol. *The Gammage Cup.* [NH 1960]

Paterson, Katherine. *Bridge to Terabithia.* [NA 1978]

Rawlings, Marjorie Kinnan. *The Secret River.* [NH 1956]

Sauer, Julia. *Fog Magic.* [NH 1944]

Sendak, Maurice. *Where the Wild Things Are.* [CA 1964]

Yorinks, Arthur. *Hey, Al.* Illus. by Richard Egielski. [CA 1987]

Imaginary playmates—Fiction

Daugherty, James. *Andy and the Lion.* [CH 1939]

Gág, Wanda. *Nothing At All.* [CH 1942]

Imagination—Fiction

Isadora, Rachel. *Ben's Trumpet.* [CH 1980]

Krauss, Ruth. *A Very Special House.* Illus. by Maurice Sendak. [CH 1954]

McGinley, Phyllis. *The Most Wonderful Doll in the World.* Illus. by Helen Stone. [CH 1951]

Ness, Evaline. *Sam, Bangs & Moonshine.* [CA 1967]

Imagination—Poetry

Seuss, Dr., pseud. (Theodor Seuss Geisel). *If I Ran the Zoo.* [CH 1951]

Seuss, Dr., pseud. (Theodor Seuss Geisel). *McElligot's Pool.* [CH 1948]

Immigrants—United States—Fiction

Estes, Eleanor. *The Hundred Dresses.* [NH 1945]

Havighurst, Walter & Marion. *Song of the Pines: A Story of Norwegian Lumbering in Wisconsin.* [NH 1950]

Lindquist, Jennie. *The Golden Name Day.* [NH 1956]

Incas—Fiction

Clark, Ann Nolan. *Secret of the Andes.* [NA 1953]

Indentured servants—Fiction

Field, Rachel. *Calico Bush.* [NH 1932]

India—Fiction

Mukerji, Dhan Gopal. *Gay Neck, the Story of a Pigeon.* [NA 1928]

Rankin, Louise. *Daughter of the Mountains.* [NH 1949]

Weston, Christine. *Bhimsa, the Dancing Bear.* [NH 1946]

India—Folklore

Brown, Marcia. *Once a Mouse.* [CA 1962]

Young, Ed. *Seven Blind Mice.* [CH 1993]

India—Kings and rulers—Biography
Eaton, Jeanette. *Gandhi, Fighter without a Sword.* **[NH 1951]**

Indian captivities—Fiction
Lenski, Lois. *Indian Captive: The Story of Mary Jemison.* **[NH 1942]**

Indian mythology—South America
Finger, Charles. *Tales from Silver Lands.* **[NA 1925]**

Indian pottery
Baylor, Byrd. *When Clay Sings.* Illus. by Tom Bahti. **[CH 1973]**

Indians of Central America—Origin
Baity, Elizabeth. *Americans Before Columbus.* **[NH 1952]**

Indians of Mexico—Fiction
Rhoads, Dorothy. *The Corn Grows Ripe.* **[NH 1957]**

Indians of Mexico—Origin
Baity, Elizabeth. *Americans Before Columbus.* **[NH 1952]**

Indians of North America
Baylor, Byrd. *When Clay Sings.* Illus. by Tom Bahti. **[CH 1973]**

Indians of North America—Fiction
Armer, Laura Adams. *Waterless Mountain.* **[NA 1932]**

Baker, Olaf. *Where the Buffaloes Begin.* Illus. by Stephen Gammell. **[CH 1982]**

Creech, Sharon. *Walk Two Moons.* **[NA 1995]**

Dalgliesh, Alice. *The Courage of Sarah Noble.* **[NH 1955]**

Hader, Berta & Elmer. *The Mighty Hunter.* **[CH 1944]**

Holling, Holling C. *Paddle-to-the-Sea.* **[CH 1942]**

Hubbard, Ralph. *Queer Person.* **[NH 1931]**

Lenski, Lois. *Indian Captive: The Story of Mary Jemison.* **[NH 1942]**

McGraw, Eloise Jarvis. *Moccasin Trail.* **[NH 1953]**

Moon, Grace. *The Runaway Papoose.* **[NH 1929]**

O'Dell, Scott. *Island of the Blue Dolphins.* **[NA 1961]**

Sandoz, Mari. *The Horsecatcher.* **[NH 1958]**

Speare, Elizabeth George. *The Sign of the Beaver.* **[NH 1984]**

Indians of North America—Folklore
Goble, Paul. *The Girl Who Loved Wild Horses.* **[CA 1979]**

Highwater, Jamake. *Anpao: An American Indian Odyssey.* **[NH 1978]**

McDermott, Gerald. *Raven: A Trickster Tale from the Pacific Northwest.* **[CH 1994]**

Sleator, William. *The Angry Moon.* Illus. by Blair Lent. **[CH 1971]**

Steptoe, John. *The Story of Jumping Mouse: A Native American Legend.* **[CH 1985]**

Indians of North America—Legends
Highwater, Jamake. *Anpao: An American Indian Odyssey.* **[NH 1978]**

McDermott, Gerald. *Arrow to the Sun: A Pueblo Indian Tale.* **[CA 1975]**

Indians of North America—Origin
Baity, Elizabeth. *Americans Before Columbus.* [NH 1952]

Indians of North America—Social life and customs
Clark, Ann Nolan. *In My Mother's House.* Illus. by Velino Herrera. [CH 1942]

Indians of North America—Southwest, New—Fiction
Miles, Miska. *Annie and the Old One.* [NH 1972]

Indians of North America—Southwest, New—History—Fiction
O'Dell, Scott. *Sing Down the Moon.* [NH 1971]

Indians of South America—Ethnic identity—Fiction
Clark, Ann Nolan. *Secret of the Andes.* [NA 1953]

Indians of South America—Fiction
Buff, Mary & Conrad. *Magic Maize.* [NH 1954]

Indians of South America—Folklore
Finger, Charles. *Tales from Silver Lands.* [NA 1925]

Indians of South America—Origin
Baity, Elizabeth. *Americans Before Columbus.* [NH 1952]

Insects—Poetry
Fleischman, Paul. *Joyful Noise: Poems for Two Voices.* [NA 1989]

Interpersonal relations—Fiction
Bunting, Eve. *Smoky Night.* Illus. by David Diaz. [CA 1995]

Horvath, Polly. *Everything on a Waffle.* [NH 2002]

Ireland—Folklore
Colum, Padraic. *The Big Tree of Bunlahy, Stories of My Own Countryside.* [NH 1934]

Young, Ella. *The Tangle-Coated Horse and Other Tales.* [NH 1930]

Young, Ella. *The Wonder Smith and His Son.* [NH 1928]

Irish Americans—Fiction
Lawson, Robert. *The Great Wheel.* [NH 1958]

Iroquois Indians—Folklore
Olds, Elizabeth. *Feather Mountain.* [CH 1952]

Islands—Fiction
L'Engle, Madeleine. *A Ring of Endless Light.* [NH 1981]

MacDonald, Golden, pseud. (Margaret Wise Brown). *The Little Island.* Illus. by Leonard Weisgard. [CA 1947]

McCloskey, Robert. *Time of Wonder.* [CA 1958]

O'Dell, Scott. *Island of the Blue Dolphins.* [NA 1961]

Parrish, Anne. *Floating Island.* [NH 1931]

Paterson, Katherine. *Jacob Have I Loved.* [NA 1981]

Robinson, Mabel Louise. *Bright Island.* [NH 1938]

Steig, William. *Abel's Island.* [NH 1977]

Tietjens, Eunice. *Boy of the South Seas.* [NH 1932]

Italian Americans—Fiction
Bartone, Elisa. *Peppe the Lamplighter.* Illus. by Ted Lewin. [CH 1994]

Italy—Folklore
Davis, Mary Gould. *The Truce of the Wolf and Other Tales of Old Italy.* [NH 1932]

de Paola, Tomie. *Strega Nona: An Old Tale.* [CH 1976]

Italy—History—Fiction
Kyle, Anne. *The Apprentice of Florence.* [NH 1934]

J

Japan—Fiction
Coatsworth, Elizabeth. *The Cat Who Went to Heaven.* [NA 1931]

Say, Allen. *Grandfather's Journey.* [CA 1994]

Yashima, Taro. *Crow Boy.* [CH 1956]

Japan—Folklore
Hodges, Margaret. *The Wave.* Illus. by Blair Lent. [CH 1965]

Mosel, Arlene. *The Funny Little Woman.* Illus. by Blair Lent. [CA 1973]

Snyder, Diane. *The Boy of the Three-Year Nap.* Illus. by Allen Say. [CH 1989]

Japan—Foreign relations—United States
Blumberg, Rhoda. *Commodore Perry in the Land of the Shogun.* [NH 1986]

Japan—Legends
Yashima, Taro. *Seashore Story.* [CH 1968]

Japan—Social life and customs—Fiction
Yashima, Taro. *Umbrella.* [CH 1959]

Japanese Americans—Evacuation and relocation, 1942–1945—Fiction
Means, Florence Crannell. *The Moved-Outers.* [NH 1946]

Japanese Americans—Fiction
Say, Allen. *Grandfather's Journey.* [CA 1994]

Jason (Greek mythology)
Colum, Padraic. *The Golden Fleece and the Heroes Who Lived before Achilles.* [NH 1922]

Jazz—Fiction
Isadora, Rachel. *Ben's Trumpet.* [CH 1980]

Weik, Mary Hays. *The Jazz Man.* [NH 1967]

Jazz musicians—Biography
Pinkney, Andrea Davis. *Duke Ellington: The Piano Prince and the Orchestra.* Illus. by Brian Pinkney. [CH 1999]

Jemison, Mary, 1743–1833—Fiction
Lenski, Lois. *Indian Captive: The Story of Mary Jemison.* [NH 1942]

Jesus Christ—Childhood
Ford, Lauren. *The Ageless Story.* [CH 1940]

Jesus Christ—Fiction
Robbins, Ruth. *Baboushka and the Three Kings.* Illus. by Nicolas Sidjakov. [CA 1961]

Speare, Elizabeth George. *The Bronze Bow.* [NA 1962]

Jews—Czech Republic—Folklore
Wisniewski, David. *Golem.* [CA 1997]

Jews—Denmark—Fiction
Lowry, Lois. *Number the Stars.* **[NA 1990]**

Jews—Folklore
McDermott, Beverly Brodsky. *The Golem: A Jewish Legend.* **[CH 1977]**

Singer, Isaac Bashevis. *When Shlemiel Went to Warsaw and Other Stories.* **[NH 1969]**

Singer, Isaac Bashevis. *Zlateh the Goat and Other Stories.* **[NH 1967]**

Taback, Simms. *Joseph Had a Little Overcoat.* **[CA 2000]**

Zemach, Margot. *It Could Always Be Worse: A Yiddish Tale.* **[CH 1978]**

Jews—Netherlands—Biography
Reiss, Johanna. *The Upstairs Room.* **[NH 1973]**

Jews—Ukraine—Berehove—Social life and customs
Siegal, Aranka. *Upon the Head of the Goat: A Childhood in Hungary, 1939–1944.* **[NH 1982]**

Jews—United States—Fiction
Ish-Kishor, Sulamith. *Our Eddie.* **[NH 1970]**

John Henry (Legendary character)
Lester, Julius. *John Henry.* Illus. by Jerry Pinkney. **[CH 1995]**

Judah Loew ben Bezalel, ca. 1525–1609—Folklore
McDermott, Beverly Brodsky. *The Golem: A Jewish Legend.* **[CH 1977]**

Wisniewski, David. *Golem.* **[CA 1997]**

Jungle animals—Fiction
Kepes, Juliet. *Five Little Monkeys.* **[CH 1953]**

Van Allsburg, Chris. *Jumanji.* **[CA 1982]**

Jungle animals—Folklore
Aardema, Verna. *Why Mosquitoes Buzz in People's Ears: A West African Tale.* Illus. by Leo & Diane Dillon. **[CA 1976]**

Juvenile delinquency—Fiction
Sachar, Louis. *Holes.* **[NA 1999]**

K

Kentucky—Fiction
Caudill, Rebecca. *Tree of Freedom.* **[NH 1950]**

Kherdian, Veron, 1907—Childhood and youth
Kherdian, David. *The Road from Home: The Story of an Armenian Girl.* **[NH 1980]**

Kidnapping—Fiction
Farmer, Nancy. *The Ear, the Eye, and the Arm.* **[NH 1995]**

Kindness—Fiction
Daugherty, James. *Andy and the Lion.* **[CH 1939]**

Freeman, Don. *Fly High, Fly Low.* **[CH 1958]**

King, Martin Luther, Jr., 1929–1968—Quotations
Rappaport, Doreen. *Martin's Big Words: The Life of Dr. Martin Luther King, Jr.* Illus. by Bryan Collier. **[CH 2002]**

Kings, queens, rulers, etc.—China—Folklore

Yolen, Jane. *The Emperor and the Kite.* Illus. by Ed Young. **[CH 1968]**

Kings, queens, rulers, etc.—Fiction

Alexander, Lloyd. *The High King.* **[NA 1969]**

de Regniers, Beatrice Schenk. *May I Bring a Friend?* Illus. by Beni Montresor. **[CA 1965]**

Elkin, Benjamin. *Gillespie and the Guards.* Illus. by James Daugherty. **[CH 1957]**

Seuss, Dr., pseud. (Theodor Seuss Geisel). *Bartholomew and the Oobleck.* **[CH 1950]**

Wood, Audrey. *King Bidgood's in the Bathtub.* Illus. by Don Wood. **[CH 1986]**

Kitchen utensils—Fiction

Dalgliesh, Alice. *The Bears on Hemlock Mountain.* **[NH 1953]**

Kites—Fiction

Wiese, Kurt. *Fish in the Air.* **[CH 1949]**

Kites—Folklore

Yolen, Jane. *The Emperor and the Kite.* Illus. by Ed Young. **[CH 1968]**

Knights and knighthood—Fiction

Lownsbery, Eloise. *Out of the Flame.* **[NH 1932]**

Marshall, Bernard G. *Cedric the Forester.* **[NH 1922]**

Knights and knighthood—Folklore

Hodges, Margaret. *Saint George and the Dragon.* Illus. by Trina Schart Hyman. **[CA 1985]**

Knossos (Extinct city)—Fiction

Berry, Erick. *The Winged Girl of Knossos.* **[NH 1934]**

Koala—Fiction

du Bois, William Pène. *Bear Party.* **[CH 1952]**

Korea—History—Koryo period, 935-1392—Fiction

Park, Linda Sue. *A Single Shard.* **[NA 2002]**

Krakatoa (Indonesia)—Eruption, 1883—Fiction

du Bois, William Pène. *The Twenty-One Balloons.* **[NA 1948]**

L

Lakes—Fiction

Enright, Elizabeth. *Gone-Away Lake.* **[NH 1958]**

Lambs—Fiction

MacDonald, Golden, pseud. (Margaret Wise Brown). *Little Lost Lamb.* Illus. by Leonard Weisgard. **[CA 1946]**

Latin America—History

Shippen, Katherine. *New Found World.* **[NH 1946]**

Lawyers—Biography

Judson, Clara Ingram. *Mr. Justice Holmes.* **[NH 1957]**

Laziness—Folklore

Snyder, Diane. *The Boy of the Three-Year Nap.* Illus. by Allen Say. **[CH 1989]**

Legends—England

Malcolmson, Anne, editor. *Song of Robin Hood.* Illus. by Virginia Lee Burton. **[CH 1948]**

Legends—Japan
Yashima, Taro. *Seashore Story.* **[CH 1968]**

Letters—Fiction
Cleary, Beverly. *Dear Mr. Henshaw.* **[NA 1984]**

Stewart, Sarah. *The Gardener.* Illus. by David Small. **[CH 1998]**

Lewis and Clark Expedition (1804–1806)—Fiction
Hewes, Agnes Danforth. *The Codfish Musket.* **[NH 1937]**

Lighthouses—Fiction
Sauer, Julia. *The Light at Tern Rock.* **[NH 1952]**

Lincoln, Abraham, 1809–1865
d'Aulaire, Ingri & Edgar Parin. *Abraham Lincoln.* **[CA 1940]**

Foster, Genevieve. *Abraham Lincoln's World.* **[NH 1945]**

Freedman, Russell. *Lincoln: A Photobiography.* **[NA 1988]**

Judson, Clara Ingram. *Abraham Lincoln, Friend of the People.* **[NH 1951]**

Lions—Fiction
Daugherty, James. *Andy and the Lion.* **[CH 1939]**

du Bois, William Pène. *Lion.* **[CH 1957]**

Literary recreations
Macaulay, David. *Black and White.* **[CA 1991]**

Little Italy (New York, N.Y.)—Fiction
Bartone, Elisa. *Peppe the Lamplighter.* Illus. by Ted Lewin. **[CH 1994]**

Locomotives—Fiction
Swift, Hildegarde Hoyt. *Little Blacknose.* **[NH 1930]**

Logging—Fiction
Meigs, Cornelia. *Swift Rivers.* **[NH 1933]**

Loneliness—Fiction
Bishop, Claire Huchet. *All Alone.* **[NH 1954]**

Snedeker, Caroline Dale. *Downright Dencey.* **[NH 1928]**

Los Angeles (Calif.)—Fiction
Politi, Leo. *Juanita.* **[CH 1949]**

Politi, Leo. *Pedro, the Angel of Olvera Street.* **[CH 1947]**

Lost and found possessions—Fiction
MacDonald, Golden, pseud. (Margaret Wise Brown). *Little Lost Lamb.* Illus. by Leonard Weisgard. **[CA 1946]**

McGinley, Phyllis. *The Most Wonderful Doll in the World.* Illus. by Helen Stone. **[CH 1951]**

Tafuri, Nancy. *Have You Seen My Duckling?* **[CH 1985]**

Will, pseud. (William Lipkind). *Finders Keepers.* Illus. by Nicolas, pseud. (Nicolas Mordvinoff). **[CA 1952]**

Lost children—Fiction
Byars, Betsy. *Summer of the Swans.* **[NA 1971]**

Lost children—Folklore
Reyher, Becky. *My Mother is the Most Beautiful Woman in the World.* Illus. by Ruth Chrisman Gannett. **[CH 1946]**

Love—Fiction
Andersen, H.C. (Hans Christian). *The Steadfast Tin Soldier.* Illus. by Marcia Brown; trans. by M.R. James. **[CH 1954]**

Paterson, Katherine. *The Great Gilly Hopkins.* **[NH 1979]**

Rylant, Cynthia. *Missing May.* **[NA 1993]**

Speare, Elizabeth George. *The Bronze Bow.* **[NA 1962]**

Luck—Folklore
Chan, Chih-Yi. *Good-Luck Horse.* Illus. by Plato Chan. **[CH 1944]**

Lullabies—Fiction
Bang, Molly. *Ten, Nine, Eight.* **[CH 1984]**

Lullabies—Poetry
Ho, Minfong. *Hush! A Thai Lullaby.* Illus. by Holly Meade. **[CH 1997]**

Lumber and lumbering—Fiction
Havighurst, Walter & Marion. *Song of the Pines: A Story of Norwegian Lumbering in Wisconsin.* **[NH 1950]**

Lynx—Fiction
Jarrell, Randall. *The Animal Family.* **[NH 1966]**

M

Madeline (Fictitious character)
Bemelmans, Ludwig. *The Golden Basket.* **[NH 1937]**

Bemelmans, Ludwig. *Madeline.* **[CH 1940]**

Bemelmans, Ludwig. *Madeline's Rescue.* **[CA 1954]**

Magic—Fiction
Alexander, Lloyd. *The Black Cauldron.* **[NH 1966]**

Alexander, Lloyd. *The High King.* **[NA 1969]**

Bond, Nancy. *A String in the Harp.* **[NH 1977]**

Bowen, William. *The Old Tobacco Shop.* **[NH 1922]**

Brittain, Bill and Andrew Glass. *The Wish Giver: Three Tales of Coven Tree.* **[NH 1984]**

Cooper, Susan. *The Dark Is Rising.* **[NH 1974]**

Cooper, Susan. *The Grey King.* **[NA 1976]**

Engdahl, Sylvia Louise. *Enchantress from the Stars.* **[NH 1971]**

Gág, Wanda. *Nothing At All.* **[CH 1942]**

Le Guin, Ursula K. *The Tombs of Atuan.* **[NH 1972]**

Sauer, Julia. *Fog Magic.* **[NH 1944]**

Snyder, Zilpha Keatley. *The Headless Cupid.* **[NH 1972]**

Steig, William. *The Amazing Bone.* **[CH 1977]**

Steig, William. *Sylvester and the Magic Pebble.* **[CA 1970]**

Turner, Megan Whalen. *The Thief.* **[NH 1997]**

Magic—Folklore
Brown, Marcia. *Once a Mouse.* **[CA 1962]**

Chan, Chih-Yi. *Good-Luck Horse.* Illus. by Plato Chan. **[CH 1944]**

Magicians—Fiction
Van Allsburg, Chris. *The Garden of Abdul Gasazi.* **[CH 1980]**

Maine—Fiction
McCloskey, Robert. *One Morning in Maine.* **[CH 1953]**

McCloskey, Robert. *Time of Wonder.* [CA 1958]

Robinson, Mabel Louise. *Bright Island.* [NH 1938]

Speare, Elizabeth George. *The Sign of the Beaver.* [NH 1984]

Maine—History—Colonial period, ca. 1600–1775—Fiction

Field, Rachel. *Calico Bush.* [NH 1932]

Man-woman relationships—Folklore

Grifalconi, Ann. *The Village of Round and Square Houses.* [CH 1987]

Maple sugar

Lasky, Kathryn. *Sugaring Time.* [NH 1984]

Marine biology—Fiction

Allee, Marjorie Hill. *Jane's Island.* [NH 1932]

Marquesas Islands (French Polynesia)—Fiction

Tietjens, Eunice. *Boy of the South Seas.* [NH 1932]

Marriage—Fiction

Staples, Suzanne Fisher. *Shabanu, Daughter of the Wind.* [NH 1990]

Martinique—Folkore

San Souci, Robert D. *The Faithful Friend.* Illus. by Brian Pinkney. [CH 1996]

Massachusetts—Fiction

Langton, Jane. *The Fledgling.* [NH 1981]

Tresselt, Alvin. *Hide and Seek Fog.* Illus. by Roger Duvoisin. [CH 1966]

Turkle, Brinton. *Thy Friend, Obadiah.* [CH 1970]

Massachusetts—History—New Plymouth, 1620–1691—Fiction

Gaggin, Eva Roe. *Down Ryton Water.* [NH 1942]

Mathematicians—Biography

Sís, Peter. *Starry Messenger: A Book Depicting the Life of a Famous Scientist, Mathematician, Astronomer, Philosopher, Physicist, Galileo Galilei.* [CH 1997]

Mayas—Ethnic identity—Fiction

Clark, Ann Nolan. *Secret of the Andes.* [NA 1953]

Mayas—Fiction

Buff, Mary & Conrad. *Magic Maize.* [NH 1954]

Malkus, Alida. *The Dark Star of Itza.* [NH 1931]

Rhoads, Dorothy. *The Corn Grows Ripe.* [NH 1957]

McKay, Donald, 1810–1880—Fiction

Sperry, Armstrong. *All Sail Set: A Romance of the Flying Cloud.* [NH 1936]

Measurement—Fiction

Lionni, Leo. *Inch by Inch.* [CH 1961]

Mediterranean Region—Civilization—Fiction

Hallock, Grace. *The Boy Who Was.* [NH 1929]

Mentally handicapped—Fiction

Byars, Betsy. *Summer of the Swans.* [NA 1971]

Martin, Ann M. *A Corner of the Universe.* [NH 2003]

Mentally ill—Fiction
Brooks, Bruce. *The Moves Make the Man.* [NH 1985]
Brooks, Bruce. *What Hearts.* [NH 1993]
Conly, Jane Leslie. *Crazy Lady.* [NH 1994]
Hamilton, Virginia. *The Planet of Junior Brown.* [NH 1972]
Hamilton, Virginia. *Sweet Whispers, Brother Rush.* [NH 1983]
Lisle, Janet Taylor. *Afternoon of the Elves.* [NH 1990]
Voigt, Cynthia. *Dicey's Song.* [NA 1983]

Meriden (Conn.)—Biography
de Paola, Tomie. *26 Fairmount Avenue.* [NH 2000]

Mermaids—Fiction
Jarrell, Randall. *The Animal Family.* [NH 1966]

Meteorologists—Biography
Martin, Jacqueline Briggs. *Snowflake Bentley.* Illus. by Mary Azarian. [CA 1999]

Metropolitan Museum of Art (New York, N.Y.)—Fiction
Konigsburg, E. L. *From the Mixed-Up Files of Mrs. Basil E. Frankweiler.* [NA 1968]

Mexico—Fiction
O'Dell, Scott. *The Black Pearl.* [NH 1968]
Rhoads, Dorothy. *The Corn Grows Ripe.* [NH 1957]

Mexico—History—Conquest, 1519-1540—Fiction
O'Dell, Scott. *The King's Fifth.* [NH 1967]

Mexico—Social life and customs—Fiction
Ets, Marie Hall and Aurora Labastida. *Nine Days to Christmas.* Illus. by Marie Hall Ets. [CA 1960]

Mice—Fiction
Henkes, Kevin. *Owen.* [CH 1994]
Lionni, Leo. *Alexander and the Wind-Up Mouse.* [CH 1970]
Lionni, Leo. *Frederick.* [CH 1968]
Low, Joseph. *Mice Twice.* [CH 1981]
O'Brien, Robert C. *Mrs. Frisby and the Rats of NIMH.* [NA 1972]
Rohmann, Eric. *My Friend Rabbit.* [CA 2003]
Selden, George, pseud. (George Thompson). *The Cricket in Times Square.* [NH 1961]
Steig, William. *Abel's Island.* [NH 1977]
Steig, William. *Doctor De Soto.* [NH 1983]
Stolz, Mary. *Belling the Tiger.* [NH 1962]
Titus, Eve. *Anatole.* Illus. by Paul Galdone. [CH 1957]
Titus, Eve. *Anatole and the Cat.* Illus. by Paul Galdone. [CH 1958]

Mice—Folklore
Steptoe, John. *The Story of Jumping Mouse: A Native American Legend.* [CH 1985]

Michigan—Fiction
Curtis, Christopher Paul. *The Watsons Go to Birmingham—1963.* [NH 1996]

Middle Ages—Fiction
Avi. *Crispin: The Cross of Lead.* [NA 2003]

Cushman, Karen. *Catherine, Called Birdy.* [NH 1995]

Cushman, Karen. *The Midwife's Apprentice.* [NA 1996]

de Angeli, Marguerite. *The Door in the Wall.* [NA 1950]

Gray, Elizabeth Janet (Elizabeth Gray Vining). *Adam of the Road.* [NA 1943]

Kelly, Eric P. *The Trumpeter of Krakow.* [NA 1929]

Midwives—Fiction

Cushman, Karen. *The Midwife's Apprentice.* [NA 1996]

Migrant labor—Fiction

Gates, Doris. *Blue Willow.* [NH 1941]

Wier, Ester. *The Loner.* [NH 1964]

Williams, Sherley Anne. *Working Cotton.* Illus. by Carole Byard. [CH 1993]

Military weapons—Fiction

Emberley, Barbara. *Drummer Hoff.* Illus. by Ed Emberley. [CA 1968]

Minnesota—Fiction

Paulsen, Gary. *The Winter Room.* [NH 1990]

Wilder, Laura Ingalls. *On the Banks of Plum Creek.* [NH 1938]

Minnesota—History—20th century—Fiction

Stong, Phil. *Honk, the Moose.* [NH 1936]

Minstrels—Fiction

Gray, Elizabeth Janet (Elizabeth Gray Vining). *Adam of the Road.* [NA 1943]

Missions—California—Fiction

Politi, Leo. *Song of the Swallows.* [CA 1950]

Mississippi—Fiction

Taylor, Mildred D. *Roll of Thunder, Hear My Cry.* [NA 1977]

Mississippi River—Fiction

Holling, Holling C. *Minn of the Mississippi.* [NH 1952]

Meigs, Cornelia. *Swift Rivers.* [NH 1933]

Modelmakers—Great Britain—Biography

Kerley, Barbara. *The Dinosaurs of Waterhouse Hawkins: An Illuminating History of Mr. Waterhouse Hawkins, Artist and Lecturer.* Illus. by Brian Selznick. [CH 2002]

Mojave Desert (Calif.)—Fiction

Schaefer, Jack. *Old Ramon.* [NH 1961]

Monasteries—Fiction

Jewett, Eleanore. *The Hidden Treasure of Glaston.* [NH 1947]

Monkeys—Fiction

Kepes, Juliet. *Five Little Monkeys.* [CH 1953]

Monsters—Fiction

Babbitt, Natalie. *Knee Knock Rise.* [NH 1971]

Sendak, Maurice. *Where the Wild Things Are.* [CA 1964]

Monsters—Poetry

Zemach, Harve. *The Judge: An Untrue Tale.* Illus. by Margot Zemach. [CH 1970]

Months—Poetry

Updike, John. *A Child's Calendar.* Illus. by Trina Schart Hyman. [CH 2000]

Moon—Fiction

Thurber, James. *Many Moons.* Illus. by Louis Slobodkin. [CA 1944]

Udry, Janice May. *The Moon Jumpers.* Illus. by Maurice Sendak. [CH 1960]

Moon—Folklore

Dayrell, Elphinstone. *Why the Sun and the Moon Live in the Sky: A Nigerian Tale.* Illus. by Blair Lent. [CH 1969]

McDermott, Gerald. *Anansi the Spider: A Tale from the Ashanti.* [CH 1973]

Moose—Fiction

Stong, Phil. *Honk, the Moose.* [NH 1936]

Morgan horse—Fiction

Henry, Marguerite. *Justin Morgan Had a Horse.* [NH 1946]

Morning—Fiction

Goudey, Alice E. *The Day We Saw the Sun Come Up.* Illus. by Adrienne Adams. [CH 1962]

Pilkey, Dav. *The Paperboy.* [CH 1997]

Mosquitoes—Folklore

Aardema, Verna. *Why Mosquitoes Buzz in People's Ears: A West African Tale.* Illus. by Leo & Diane Dillon. [CA 1976]

Mother Goose

de Angeli, Marguerite. *Book of Nursery and Mother Goose Rhymes.* [CH 1955]

Reed, Philip. *Mother Goose and Nursery Rhymes.* [CH 1964]

Tudor, Tasha. *Mother Goose.* [CH 1945]

Wheeler, Opal. *Sing Mother Goose.* Illus. by Marjorie Torrey. [CH 1946]

Mothers—Fiction

McCloskey, Robert. *Blueberries for Sal.* [CH 1949]

Mothers—Folklore

Reyher, Becky. *My Mother is the Most Beautiful Woman in the World.* Illus. by Ruth Chrisman Gannett. [CH 1946]

Mothers and daughters—Fiction

Dalgliesh, Alice. *The Silver Pencil.* [NH 1945]

McCloskey, Robert. *Blueberries for Sal.* [CH 1949]

Williams, Vera B. *A Chair for My Mother.* [CH 1983]

Mothers and sons—Fiction

Brooks, Bruce. *What Hearts.* [NH 1993]

Coman, Carolyn. *What Jamie Saw.* [NH 1996]

Edmonds, Walter Dumaux. *The Matchlock Gun.* [NA 1942]

Lewis, Elizabeth Foreman. *Young Fu of the Upper Yangtze.* [NA 1933]

Shannon, Monica. *Dobry.* [NA 1935]

Mothers and sons—Folklore

Snyder, Diane. *The Boy of the Three-Year Nap.* Illus. by Allen Say. [CH 1989]

Mountain life—Fiction

Dalgliesh, Alice. *The Bears on Hemlock Mountain.* [NH 1953]

George, Jean Craighead. *My Side of the Mountain.* [NH 1960]

Kendall, Carol. *The Gammage Cup.* [NH 1960]

Rylant, Cynthia. *When I Was Young in the Mountains*. Illus. by Diane Goode. **[CH 1983]**

Mountain life—France—Fiction
Bishop, Claire Huchet. *All Alone*. **[NH 1954]**

Mountain life—Peru—Fiction
Clark, Ann Nolan. *Secret of the Andes*. **[NA 1953]**

Mountaineering—Fiction
Ullman, James Ramsey. *Banner in the Sky*. **[NH 1955]**

Mountains—Fiction
Hamilton, Virginia. *M.C. Higgins, the Great*. **[NA 1975]**

Moving, Household—Fiction
Barnes, Nancy. *Wonderful Year*. **[NH 1947]**

Estes, Eleanor. *The Middle Moffat*. **[NH 1943]**

Fenner, Carol. *Yolonda's Genius*. **[NH 1996]**

Mozambique—Fiction
Farmer, Nancy. *A Girl Named Disaster*. **[NH 1997]**

Murder—Fiction
Raskin, Ellen. *The Westing Game*. **[NA 1979]**

Snyder, Zilpha Keatley. *The Egypt Game*. **[NH 1968]**

Yep, Laurence. *Dragonwings*. **[NH 1976]**

Museums—Fiction
Konigsburg, E. L. *From the Mixed-Up Files of Mrs. Basil E. Frankweiler*. **[NA 1968]**

Rohmann, Eric. *Time Flies*. **[CH 1995]**

Music—Fiction
Moss, Lloyd. *Zin! Zin! Zin! A Violin*. Illus. by Marjorie Priceman. **[CH 1996]**

Music—History and criticism
Wheeler, Opal. *Sing in Praise: A Collection of the Best Loved Hymns*. Illus. by Marjorie Torrey. **[CH 1947]**

Musical instruments—Fiction
Moss, Lloyd. *Zin! Zin! Zin! A Violin*. Illus. by Marjorie Priceman. **[CH 1996]**

Musicians—Biography
Pinkney, Andrea Davis. *Duke Ellington: The Piano Prince and the Orchestra*. Illus. by Brian Pinkney. **[CH 1999]**

Musicians—Fiction
Fenner, Carol. *Yolonda's Genius*. **[NH 1996]**

Isadora, Rachel. *Ben's Trumpet*. **[CH 1980]**

Weik, Mary Hays. *The Jazz Man*. **[NH 1967]**

Musicians—Folklore
Plume, Ilse. *The Bremen-Town Musicians*. Adapted from the Brothers Grimm. **[CH 1981]**

Mutiny—Fiction
Avi. *The True Confessions of Charlotte Doyle*. **[NH 1991]**

Mutism—Fiction
Hubbard, Ralph. *Queer Person*. **[NH 1931]**

Mystery fiction
Estes, Eleanor. *Ginger Pye*. **[NA 1952]**

Farmer, Nancy. *The Ear, the Eye, and the Arm.* **[NH 1995]**

Konigsburg, E. L. *From the Mixed-Up Files of Mrs. Basil E. Frankweiler.* **[NA 1968]**

McGraw, Eloise Jarvis. *The Golden Goblet.* **[NH 1962]**

Raskin, Ellen. *The Westing Game.* **[NA 1979]**

Mythology

Hamilton, Virginia. *In the Beginning: Creation Stories from Around the World.* **[NH 1989]**

Mythology, Chinese

Seeger, Elizabeth. *The Pageant of Chinese History.* **[NH 1935]**

Mythology, Greek

Colum, Padraic. *The Golden Fleece and the Heroes Who Lived before Achilles.* **[NH 1922]**

N

Nansen, Fridtjof, 1861-1930

Hall, Anna Gertrude. *Nansen.* **[NH 1941]**

Nantucket Island (Mass.)—Fiction

Turkle, Brinton. *Thy Friend, Obadiah.* **[CH 1970]**

Nantucket Island (Mass.)—19th century—Fiction

Snedeker, Caroline Dale. *Downright Dencey.* **[NH 1928]**

Nathaniel Bowditch, 1773-1838—Fiction

Latham, Jean Lee. *Carry On, Mr. Bowditch.* **[NA 1956]**

Natural history

Shippen, Katherine B. *Men, Microscopes, and Living Things.* **[NH 1956]**

Naturalists—Biography

Robinson, Mabel Louise. *Runner of the Mountain Tops: The Life of Louis Agassiz.* **[NH 1940]**

Naturalists—Fiction

Allee, Marjorie Hill. *Jane's Island.* **[NH 1932]**

Nature

Lasky, Kathryn. *Sugaring Time.* **[NH 1984]**

Udry, Janice May. *A Tree Is Nice.* Illus. by Marc Simont. **[CA 1957]**

Nature—Fiction

Buff, Mary & Conrad. *Big Tree.* **[NH 1947]**

Buff, Mary & Conrad. *Dash and Dart.* **[CH 1943]**

Dalgliesh, Alice. *The Bears on Hemlock Mountain.* **[NH 1953]**

Fleming, Denise. *In the Small, Small Pond.* **[CH 1994]**

Goudey, Alice E. *The Day We Saw the Sun Come Up.* Illus. by Adrienne Adams. **[CH 1962]**

McCloskey, Robert. *Time of Wonder.* **[CA 1958]**

Paulsen, Gary. *Hatchet.* **[NH 1988]**

Sorensen, Virginia. *Miracles on Maple Hill.* **[NA 1957]**

Yolen, Jane. *Owl Moon.* Illus. by John Schoenherr. **[CA 1988]**

Nature—Folklore

Belting, Natalia M. *The Sun Is a Golden Earring.* Illus. by Bernarda Bryson. **[CH 1963]**

Dayrell, Elphinstone. *Why the Sun and the Moon Live in the Sky: A Nigerian Tale.* Illus. by Blair Lent. **[CH 1969]**

McDermott, Gerald. *Anansi the Spider: A Tale from the Ashanti.* **[CH 1973]**

Nature photography

Martin, Jacqueline Briggs. *Snowflake Bentley.* Illus. by Mary Azarian. **[CA 1999]**

Nature study—Fiction

Allee, Marjorie Hill. *Jane's Island.* **[NH 1932]**

Navajo Indians—Fiction

Miles, Miska. *Annie and the Old One.* **[NH 1972]**

Navajo Indians—History—Fiction

O'Dell, Scott. *Sing Down the Moon.* **[NH 1971]**

Navajo Indians—Social life and customs—Fiction

Armer, Laura Adams. *Waterless Mountain.* **[NA 1932]**

Navigation—Fiction

Latham, Jean Lee. *Carry On, Mr. Bowditch.* **[NA 1956]**

Neighbors—Fiction

Bunting, Eve. *Smoky Night.* Illus. by David Diaz. **[CA 1995]**

Lenski, Lois. *Strawberry Girl.* **[NA 1946]**

Montgomery, Rutherford. *Kildee House.* **[NH 1950]**

Sawyer, Ruth. *Roller Skates.* **[NA 1937]**

Netherlands—Fiction

Van Stockum, Hilda. *A Day on Skates: The Story of a Dutch Picnic.* **[NH 1935]**

Netherlands—History—German occupation, 1940–1945

Reiss, Johanna. *The Upstairs Room.* **[NH 1973]**

New England—Fiction

Coblentz, Catherine. *The Blue Cat of Castle Town.* **[NH 1950]**

Hall, Donald. *Ox-Cart Man.* Illus. by Barbara Cooney. **[CA 1980]**

Meigs, Cornelia. *The Windy Hill.* **[NH 1922]**

Spier, Peter. *Fox Went Out on a Chilly Night: An Old Song.* **[CH 1962]**

New England—History—1775–1865—Fiction

Meigs, Cornelia. *Clearing Weather.* **[NH 1929]**

New England—History—Colonial period, ca. 1600–1775—Fiction

Hewes, Agnes Danforth. *The Codfish Musket.* **[NH 1937]**

New Hampshire—Fiction

Bailey, Carolyn Sherwin. *Miss Hickory.* **[NA 1947]**

New Hampshire—History—Fiction

Blos, Joan W. *A Gathering of Days: A New England Girl's Journal, 1830–1832.* **[NA 1980]**

New Mexico—Fiction

Krumgold, Joseph. *... And Now Miguel.* **[NA 1954]**

New Providence (R.I.)—History—Colonial Period, ca.1600–1775
Eaton, Jeanette. *Lone Journey: The Life of Roger Williams.* [NH 1945]

New York (N.Y.)—Fiction
Bartone, Elisa. *Peppe the Lamplighter.* Illus. by Ted Lewin. [CH 1994]

Cleary, Beverly. *Dear Mr. Henshaw.* [NA 1984]

Konigsburg, E. L. *From the Mixed-Up Files of Mrs. Basil E. Frankweiler.* [NA 1968]

Moore, Annie Carroll. *Nicholas: A Manhattan Christmas Story.* [NH 1925]

Neville, Emily. *It's Like This, Cat.* [NA 1964]

Sawyer, Ruth. *Roller Skates.* [NA 1937]

Stolz, Mary. *The Noonday Friends.* [NH 1966]

New York (State)—Fiction
Giff, Patricia Reilly. *Pictures of Hollis Woods.* [NH 2003]

Newspaper carriers—Fiction
Pilkey, Dav. *The Paperboy.* [CH 1997]

Nigeria—Fiction
Best, Herbert. *Garram the Hunter: A Boy of the Hill Tribes.* [NH 1931]

Nigeria—Folklore
Dayrell, Elphinstone. *Why the Sun and the Moon Live in the Sky: A Nigerian Tale.* Illus. by Blair Lent. [CH 1969]

Night—Fiction
Brown, Margaret Wise. *A Child's Good Night Book.* Illus. by Jean Charlot. [CH 1944]

Ryan, Cheli Duran. *Hildilid's Night.* Illus. Arnold Lobel. [CH 1972]

Udry, Janice May. *The Moon Jumpers.* Illus. by Maurice Sendak. [CH 1960]

Noah (Biblical figure)
Pinkney, Jerry. *Noah's Ark.* [CH 2003]

Noah's ark
Pinkney, Jerry. *Noah's Ark.* [CH 2003]

Spier, Peter. *Noah's Ark.* [CA 1978]

Noah's ark—Songs and music
Emberley, Barbara. *One Wide River to Cross.* Illus. by Ed Emberley. [CH 1967]

Nonsense verse
Eichenberg, Fritz. *Ape in a Cape: An Alphabet of Odd Animals.* [CH 1953]

Emberley, Barbara. *One Wide River to Cross.* Illus. by Ed Emberley. [CH 1967]

Preston, Edna Mitchell. *Pop Corn & Ma Goodness.* Illus. by Robert Andrew Parker. [CH 1970]

Scheer, Julian. *Rain Makes Applesauce.* Illus. by Marvin Bileck. [CH 1965]

Seuss, Dr., pseud. (Theodor Seuss Geisel). *If I Ran the Zoo.* [CH 1951]

Seuss, Dr., pseud. (Theodor Seuss Geisel). *McElligot's Pool.* [CH 1948]

Taback, Simms. *There Was an Old Lady Who Swallowed a Fly.* [CH 1998]

Nonviolence
Eaton, Jeanette. *Gandhi, Fighter without a Sword.* [NH 1951]

North Carolina—Fiction
Rylant, Cynthia. *A Fine White Dust.* [NH 1987]

Tolan, Stephanie S. *Surviving the Applewhites.* [NH 2003]

North Carolina—History—Revolution, 1775–1783—Fiction
Gray, Elizabeth Janet (Elizabeth Gray Vining). *Meggy MacIntosh.* [NH 1931]

North Pole—Fiction
Van Allsburg, Chris. *The Polar Express.* [CA 1986]

North, Sterling, 1906–1974—Childhood and youth
North, Sterling. *Rascal: A Memoir of a Better Era.* [NH 1964]

Northwest, Pacific—Folklore
McDermott, Gerald. *Raven: A Trickster Tale from the Pacific Northwest.* [CH 1994]

Norwegian Americans—Fiction
Havighurst, Walter & Marion. *Song of the Pines: A Story of Norwegian Lumbering in Wisconsin.* [NH 1950]

Paulsen, Gary. *The Winter Room.* [NH 1990]

Nova Scotia—Fiction
Sauer, Julia. *Fog Magic.* [NH 1944]

Numerals
Feelings, Muriel. *Moja Means One: Swahili Counting Book.* Illus. by Tom Feelings. [CH 1972]

Tudor, Tasha. *1 Is One.* [CH 1957]

Nursery rhymes
de Angeli, Marguerite. *Book of Nursery and Mother Goose Rhymes.* [CH 1955]

Domanska, Janina. *If All the Seas Were One Sea.* [CH 1972]

Fish, Helen Dean. *Four and Twenty Blackbirds.* Illus. by Robert Lawson. [CH 1938]

Frasconi, Antonio. *The House That Jack Built: La Maison Que Jacques A Batie.* [CH 1959]

Jeffers, Susan. *Three Jovial Huntsmen.* [CH 1974]

Petersham, Maude & Miska. *The Rooster Crows: A Book of American Rhymes and Jingles.* [CA 1946]

Reed, Philip. *Mother Goose and Nursery Rhymes.* [CH 1964]

Tudor, Tasha. *Mother Goose.* [CH 1945]

Wheeler, Opal. *Sing Mother Goose.* Illus. by Marjorie Torrey. [CH 1946]

O

Obedience—Fiction
Bauer, Marion Dane. *On My Honor.* [NH 1987]

Staples, Suzanne Fisher. *Shabanu, Daughter of the Wind.* [NH 1990]

Occultism—Fiction
Fleischman, Paul and Andrew Glass. *Graven Images.* [NH 1983]

Ocean voyages—Fiction
Creech, Sharon. *The Wanderer.* [NH 2001]

Ocean waves—Folklore
Hodges, Margaret. *The Wave.* Illus. by Blair Lent. [CH 1965]

Ohio—Fiction
Hamilton, Virginia. *M. C. Higgins, the Great.* [NA 1975]

Ohio River—Fiction
Crawford, Phyllis. *"Hello, the Boat!"* [NH 1939]

Ohio River Valley—History—Fiction
Hewes, Agnes Danforth. *The Codfish Musket.* [NH 1937]

Oklahoma—Fiction
Hesse, Karen. *Out of the Dust.* [NA 1998]

Orchestra—Fiction
Moss, Lloyd. *Zin! Zin! Zin! A Violin.* Illus. by Marjorie Priceman. [CH 1996]

Oregon—Fiction
Cleary, Beverly. *Ramona and Her Father.* [NH 1978]

Cleary, Beverly. *Ramona Quimby, Age 8.* [NH 1982]

Orphans—Fiction
Avi. *Crispin: The Cross of Lead.* [NA 2003]

Davis, Julia. *Mountains Are Free.* [NH 1931]

Field, Rachel. *Calico Bush.* [NH 1932]

Giff, Patricia Reilly. *Pictures of Hollis Woods.* [NH 2003]

Gray, Elizabeth Janet (Elizabeth Gray Vining). *Meggy MacIntosh.* [NH 1931]

Havighurst, Walter & Marion. *Song of the Pines: A Story of Norwegian Lumbering in Wisconsin.* [NH 1950]

Hawes, Charles. *The Dark Frigate.* [NA 1924]

Meigs, Cornelia. *Swift Rivers.* [NH 1933]

Park, Linda Sue. *A Single Shard.* [NA 2002]

Spinelli, Jerry. *Maniac Magee.* [NA 1991]

Wier, Ester. *The Loner.* [NH 1964]

Owls—Fiction
Hiaasen, Carl. *Hoot.* [NH 2003]

Yolen, Jane. *Owl Moon.* Illus. by John Schoenherr. [CA 1988]

P

Paine, Thomas, 1737–1809
Gurko, Leo. *Tom Paine, Freedom's Apostle.* [NH 1958]

Painting, Modern—19th century—United States
Rourke, Constance. *Audubon.* [NH 1937]

Pakistan—Fiction
Staples, Suzanne Fisher. *Shabanu, Daughter of the Wind.* [NH 1990]

Palestine—Fiction
Speare, Elizabeth George. *The Bronze Bow.* [NA 1962]

Pampas (Argentina)—Fiction
Kalnay, Francis. *Chucaro: Wild Pony of the Pampa.* [NH 1959]

Pancakes, waffles, etc.—Fiction
Bishop, Claire Huchet. *Pancakes-Paris.* [NH 1948]

Pancakes, waffles, etc.—Folklore
Sawyer, Ruth. *Journey Cake, Ho!* Illus. by Robert McCloskey. [CH 1954]

Parades—Fiction
Politi, Leo. *Juanita*. [CH 1949]

Paradise—Fiction
Yorinks, Arthur. *Hey, Al*. Illus. by Richard Egielski. [CA 1987]

Pareja, Juan de, 1606–1670—Fiction
Trevino, Elizabeth Borton de. *I, Juan de Pareja*. [NA 1966]

Parent and child—Fiction
Brooks, Bruce. *What Hearts*. [NH 1993]

Cleary, Beverly. *Dear Mr. Henshaw*. [NA 1984]

Henkes, Kevin. *Owen*. [CH 1994]

Horvath, Polly. *Everything on a Waffle*. [NH 2002]

Williams, Vera B. *"More More More," Said the Baby: Three Love Stories*. [CH 1991]

Parent-teacher relationships—Fiction
Avi. *Nothing but the Truth: A Documentary Novel*. [NH 1992]

Parents—Fiction
Macaulay, David. *Black and White*. [CA 1991]

Paris (France)—Fiction
Bemelmans, Ludwig. *Madeline*. [CH 1940]

Bemelmans, Ludwig. *Madeline's Rescue*. [CA 1954]

Carlson, Natalie Savage. *The Family under the Bridge*. [NH 1959]

McCully, Emily Arnold. *Mirette on the High Wire*. [CA 1993]

Titus, Eve. *Anatole*. Illus. by Paul Galdone. [CH 1957]

Titus, Eve. *Anatole and the Cat*. Illus. by Paul Galdone. [CH 1958]

Parties—Fiction
du Bois, William Pène. *Bear Party*. [CH 1952]

Patriotism—Fiction
Davis, Julia. *Vaino: A Boy of New Finland*. [NH 1930]

Patriotism in art
Petersham, Maud & Miska. *An American ABC*. [CH 1942]

Pearl diving—Fiction
O'Dell, Scott. *The Black Pearl*. [NH 1968]

Pecos Bill (Legendary character)
Bowman, James Cloyd. *Pecos Bill, the Greatest Cowboy of All Times*. [NH 1938]

Peet, Bill
Peet, Bill. *Bill Peet: An Autobiography*. [CH 1990]

Penguins—Fiction
Atwater, Richard. *Mr. Popper's Penguins*. [NH 1939]

Penn, William, 1644–1718
Gray, Elizabeth Janet (Elizabeth Gray Vining). *Penn*. [NH 1939]

Pennsylvania—Fiction
Sorensen, Virginia. *Miracles on Maple Hill*. [NA 1957]

Pennsylvania—History—Colonial period, ca. 1600–1775
Gray, Elizabeth Janet (Elizabeth Gray Vining). *Penn*. [NH 1939]

Pennsylvania Dutch—Fiction
de Angeli, Marguerite. *Yonie Wondernose.* [CH 1945]

Milhous, Katherine. *The Egg Tree.* [CA 1951]

Perry, Matthew Calbraith, 1794–1858
Blumberg, Rhoda. *Commodore Perry in the Land of the Shogun.* [NH 1986]

Peru—Fiction
Clark, Ann Nolan. *Secret of the Andes.* [NA 1953]

Pets—Fiction
DeJong, Meindert. *Hurry Home, Candy.* [NH 1954]

DeJong, Meindert. *Shadrach.* [NH 1954]

McCarty, Peter. *Hondo & Fabian.* [CH 2003]

Philosophers—Biography
Sís, Peter. *Starry Messenger: A Book Depicting the Life of a Famous Scientist, Mathematician, Astronomer, Philosopher, Physicist, Galileo Galilei.* [CH 1997]

Photographers—Biography
Martin, Jacqueline Briggs. *Snowflake Bentley.* Illus. by Mary Azarian. [CA 1999]

Physicists—Biography
Sís, Peter. *Starry Messenger: A Book Depicting the Life of a Famous Scientist, Mathematician, Astronomer, Philosopher, Physicist, Galileo Galilei.* [CH 1997]

Piano music
Wheeler, Opal. *Sing in Praise: A Collection of the Best Loved Hymns.* Illus. by Marjorie Torrey. [CH 1947]

Pianists—Biography
Pinkney, Andrea Davis. *Duke Ellington: The Piano Prince and the Orchestra.* Illus. by Brian Pinkney. [CH 1999]

Picnicking—Fiction
Van Stockum, Hilda. *A Day on Skates: The Story of a Dutch Picnic.* [NH 1935]

Pigeons—Fiction
Freeman, Don. *Fly High, Fly Low.* [CH 1958]

Mukerji, Dhan Gopal. *Gay Neck, the Story of a Pigeon.* [NA 1928]

Spinelli, Jerry. *Wringer.* [NH 1998]

Pigs—Fiction
Falconer, Ian. *Olivia.* [CH 2001]

Steig, William. *The Amazing Bone.* [CH 1977]

White, E. B. *Charlotte's Web.* [NH 1952]

Wiesner, David. *The Three Pigs.* [CA 2002]

Pilgrims (New Plymouth Colony)—Fiction
Dalgliesh, Alice. *The Thanksgiving Story.* Illus. by Helen Sewell. [CH 1955]

Gaggin, Eva Roe. *Down Ryton Water.* [NH 1942]

Pioneers—Biography
Lawson, Robert. *They Were Strong and Good.* [CA 1941]

Pioneers—Pennsylvania—Biography
Gray, Elizabeth Janet (Elizabeth Gray Vining). *Penn.* [NH 1939]

Pioneers—Tennessee—Biography
Daugherty, James. *Daniel Boone.* [NA 1940]
Rourke, Constance. *Davy Crockett.* [NH 1935]

Pioneers—West (U.S.)
Tunis, Edwin. *Frontier Living.* [NH 1962]

Pirates—Fiction
Hawes, Charles. *The Dark Frigate.* [NA 1924]
Hewes, Agnes Danforth. *Spice and the Devil's Cave.* [NH 1931]
Lownsbery, Eloise. *Out of the Flame.* [NH 1932]

Play—Fiction
Ets, Marie Hall. *Just Me.* [CH 1966]
Udry, Janice May. *The Moon Jumpers.* Illus. by Maurice Sendak. [CH 1960]
Van Allsburg, Chris. *Jumanji.* [CA 1982]

Plymouth (Mass.)—History—Fiction
Dalgliesh, Alice. *The Thanksgiving Story.* Illus. by Helen Sewell. [CH 1955]

Poetry
Cendrars, Blaise. *Shadow.* Illus. and trans. by Marcia Brown. [CA 1983]
de Angeli, Marguerite. *Book of Nursery and Mother Goose Rhymes.* [CH 1955]
Domanska, Janina. *If All the Seas Were One Sea.* [CH 1972]
Fish, Helen Dean. *Four and Twenty Blackbirds.* Illus. by Robert Lawson. [CH 1938]
Fleischman, Paul. *Joyful Noise: Poems for Two Voices.* [NA 1989]
Frasconi, Antonio. *The House That Jack Built: La Maison Que Jacques A Batie.* [CH 1959]
Howitt, Mary. *The Spider and the Fly.* Illus. by Tony DiTerlizzi. [CH 2003]
Jeffers, Susan. *Three Jovial Huntsmen.* [CH 1974]
McGinley, Phyllis. *All Around the Town.* Illus. by Helen Stone. [CH 1949]
Myers, Walter Dean. *Harlem.* Illus. by Christopher Myers. [CH 1998]
Nelson, Marilyn. *Carver: A Life in Poems.* [NH 2002]
Petersham, Maude & Miska. *The Rooster Crows: A Book of American Rhymes and Jingles.* [CA 1946]
Reed, Philip. *Mother Goose and Nursery Rhymes.* [CH 1964]
Thayer, Ernest Lawrence. *Casey at the Bat: A Ballad of the Republic Sung in the Year 1888.* Illus. by Christopher Bing. [CH 2001]
Tudor, Tasha. *Mother Goose.* [CH 1945]
Updike, John. *A Child's Calendar.* Illus. by Trina Schart Hyman. [CH 2000]
Wheeler, Opal. *Sing Mother Goose.* Illus. by Marjorie Torrey. [CH 1946]
Willard, Nancy. *A Visit to William Blake's Inn: Poems for Innocent and Experienced Travelers.* [NA 1982, CH 1982]

Poetry—Fiction
Hesse, Karen. *Out of the Dust.* [NA 1998]

Poets—Fiction
Lionni, Leo. *Frederick.* **[CH 1968]**

Poland—Fiction
Singer, Isaac Bashevis. *The Fearsome Inn.* **[NH 1968]**

Poland—Folklore
Singer, Isaac Bashevis. *When Shlemiel Went to Warsaw and Other Stories.* **[NH 1969]**

Singer, Isaac Bashevis. *Zlateh the Goat and Other Stories.* **[NH 1967]**

Poland—History—Casimir IV, 1447–1492—Fiction
Kelly, Eric P. *The Trumpeter of Krakow.* **[NA 1929]**

Polar region—Fiction
Van Allsburg, Chris. *The Polar Express.* **[CA 1986]**

Police—Fiction
Rathmann, Peggy. *Officer Buckle and Gloria.* **[CA 1996]**

Police dogs—Fiction
Rathmann, Peggy. *Officer Buckle and Gloria.* **[CA 1996]**

Polish Americans—Fiction
Estes, Eleanor. *The Hundred Dresses.* **[NH 1945]**

Politics, Practical—Fiction
Bauer, Joan. *Hope Was Here.* **[NH 2001]**

Polynesia—Fiction
Sperry, Armstrong. *Call It Courage.* **[NA 1941]**

Ponds—Fiction
Fleming, Denise. *In the Small, Small Pond.* **[CH 1994]**

Seuss, Dr., pseud. (Theodor Seuss Geisel). *McElligot's Pool.* **[CH 1948]**

Tafuri, Nancy. *Have You Seen My Duckling?* **[CH 1985]**

Ponies—Fiction
Henry, Marguerite. *Misty of Chincoteague.* **[NH 1948]**

Kalnay, Francis. *Chucaro: Wild Pony of the Pampa.* **[NH 1959]**

Portugal—Territorial expansion—Fiction
Hewes, Agnes Danforth. *Spice and the Devil's Cave.* **[NH 1931]**

Posadas (Social custom)—Fiction
Ets, Marie Hall and Aurora Labastida. *Nine Days to Christmas.* Illus. by Marie Hall Ets. **[CA 1960]**

Politi, Leo. *Pedro, the Angel of Olvera Street.* **[CH 1947]**

Pottery
Baylor, Byrd. *When Clay Sings.* Illus. by Tom Bahti. **[CH 1973]**

Pottery—Fiction
Park, Linda Sue. *A Single Shard.* **[NA 2002]**

Poverty—Fiction
Armstrong, William H. *Sounder.* **[NA 1970]**

Taylor, Mildred D. *Roll of Thunder, Hear My Cry.* **[NA 1977]**

Weik, Mary Hays. *The Jazz Man.* **[NH 1967]**

Prague (Czech Republic)—Folklore
Wisniewski, David. *Golem.* **[CA 1997]**

Prairies—Fiction
MacLachlan, Patricia. *Sarah, Plain and Tall.* [NA 1986]

Prayer-books and devotions
Field, Rachel. *Prayer for a Child.* Illus. by Elizabeth Orton Jones. [CA 1945]

Prayers
Field, Rachel. *Prayer for a Child.* Illus. by Elizabeth Orton Jones. [CA 1945]

Prayers for animals—Fiction
Politi, Leo. *Juanita.* [CH 1949]

Prejudices—Fiction
Armstrong, William H. *Sounder.* [NA 1970]

Curtis, Christopher Paul. *The Watsons Go to Birmingham—1963.* [NH 1996]

Hamilton, Virginia. *M. C. Higgins, the Great.* [NA 1975]

Means, Florence Crannell. *The Moved-Outers.* [NH 1946]

Spinelli, Jerry. *Maniac Magee.* [NA 1991]

Taylor, Mildred D. *Roll of Thunder, Hear My Cry.* [NA 1977]

Presidents—United States—Biography
d'Aulaire, Ingri & Edgar Parin. *Abraham Lincoln.* [CA 1940]

Eaton, Jeanette. *Leader by Destiny: George Washington, Man and Patriot.* [NH 1939]

Foster, Genevieve. *Abraham Lincoln's World.* [NH 1945]

Foster, Genevieve. *George Washington.* [NH 1950]

Foster, Genevieve. *George Washington's World.* [NH 1942]

Freedman, Russell. *Lincoln: A Photobiography.* [NA 1988]

Judson, Clara Ingram. *Abraham Lincoln, Friend of the People.* [NH 1951]

Judson, Clara Ingram. *Theodore Roosevelt, Fighting Patriot.* [NH 1954]

St. George, Judith. *So You Want to Be President?* Illus. by David Small. [CA 2001]

Presidents—United States—Family—Biography
Freedman, Russell. *Eleanor Roosevelt: A Life of Discovery.* [NH 1994]

Presidents' spouses—United States—Biography
Freedman, Russell. *Eleanor Roosevelt: A Life of Discovery.* [NH 1994]

Princesses—Fiction
Thurber, James. *Many Moons.* Illus. by Louis Slobodkin. [CA 1944]

Prisoners—Fiction
Myers, Walter Dean. *Somewhere in the Darkness.* [NH 1993]

Sachar, Louis. *Holes.* [NA 1999]

Prisoners of war—Fiction
Keith, Harold. *Rifles for Watie.* [NA 1958]

Sorensen, Virginia. *Miracles on Maple Hill.* [NA 1957]

Prohibition
Johnson, Gerald W. *America Moves Forward: A History for Peter.* [NH 1961]

Pueblo Indians—Legends
McDermott, Gerald. *Arrow to the Sun: A Pueblo Indian Tale.* [CA 1975]

Pueblos

Clark, Ann Nolan. *In My Mother's House.* Illus. by Velino Herrera. **[CH 1942]**

Puritans—Fiction

Speare, Elizabeth George. *The Witch of Blackbird Pond.* **[NA 1959]**

Q

Quakers—Fiction

Snedeker, Caroline Dale. *Downright Dencey.* **[NH 1928]**

Turkle, Brinton. *Thy Friend, Obadiah.* **[CH 1970]**

Quakers—Pennsylvania—Biography

Gray, Elizabeth Janet (Elizabeth Gray Vining). *Penn.* **[NH 1939]**

Quimby, Ramona (Ficticious Character)

Cleary, Beverly. *Ramona and Her Father.* **[NH 1978]**

Cleary, Beverly. *Ramona Quimby, Age 8.* **[NH 1982]**

R

Rabbits—Fiction

DeJong, Meindert. *Shadrach.* **[NH 1954]**

Gág, Wanda. *The ABC Bunny.* **[NH 1934]**

Lawson, Robert. *Rabbit Hill.* **[NA 1945]**

Newberry, Clare Turlay. *Marshmallow.* **[CH 1943]**

Rohmann, Eric. *My Friend Rabbit.* **[CA 2003]**

Schlein, Miriam. *When Will the World Be Mine?* Illus. by Jean Charlot. **[CH 1954]**

Zolotow, Charlotte. *Mr. Rabbit and the Lovely Present.* Illus. by Maurice Sendak. **[CH 1963]**

Rabbits—Folklore

Stevens, Janet. *Tops & Bottoms.* **[CH 1996]**

Raccoons

North, Sterling. *Rascal: A Memoir of a Better Era.* **[NH 1964]**

Raccoons—Fiction

Montgomery, Rutherford. *Kildee House.* **[NH 1950]**

Race relations—Fiction

Brooks, Bruce. *The Moves Make the Man.* **[NH 1985]**

Bunting, Eve. *Smoky Night.* Illus. by David Diaz. **[CA 1995]**

Raschka, Christopher. *Yo! Yes?* **[CH 1994]**

Spinelli, Jerry. *Maniac Magee.* **[NA 1991]**

Race relations—Folklore

San Souci, Robert D. *The Faithful Friend.* Illus. by Brian Pinkney. **[CH 1996]**

Railroads—Trains

Crews, Donald. *Freight Train.* **[CH 1979]**

Railroads—Trains—Fiction

Macaulay, David. *Black and White.* **[CA 1991]**

Swift, Hildegarde Hoyt. *Little Blacknose.* **[NH 1930]**

Van Allsburg, Chris. *The Polar Express.* **[CA 1986]**

Railroads—West (U.S.)—History—Fiction
Yep, Laurence. *Dragon's Gate.* [NH 1994]

Rain and rainfall—Fiction
Tresselt, Alvin. *Rain Drop Splash.* Illus. by Leonard Weisgard. [CH 1947]

Yashima, Taro. *Umbrella.* [CH 1959]

Zolotow, Charlotte. *The Storm Book.* Illus. by Margaret Bloy Graham. [CH 1953]

Rain forests—Fiction
Armer, Laura Adams. *The Forest Pool.* [CH 1939]

Rams—Fiction
Kalashnikoff, Nicholas. *The Defender.* [NH 1952]

Ranch life—Montana—Fiction
Wier, Ester. *The Loner.* [NH 1964]

Rats—Fiction
O'Brien, Robert C. *Mrs. Frisby and the Rats of NIMH.* [NA 1972]

Rays (Fishes)—Fiction
O'Dell, Scott. *The Black Pearl.* [NH 1968]

Refugees—Fiction
Giff, Patricia Reilly. *Lily's Crossing.* [NH 1998]

Reiss, Johanna
Reiss, Johanna. *The Upstairs Room.* [NH 1973]

Rejection (Psychology)—Fiction
Estes, Eleanor. *The Hundred Dresses.* [NH 1945]

Kendall, Carol. *The Gammage Cup.* [NH 1960]

Pinkney, Jerry. *The Ugly Duckling.* Adapted from Hans Christian Andersen. [CH 2000]

Raskin, Ellen. *Figgs & Phantoms.* [NH 1975]

Sandoz, Mari. *The Horsecatcher.* [NH 1958]

Yashima, Taro. *Crow Boy.* [CH 1956]

Religious leaders—Biography
Eaton, Jeanette. *Lone Journey: The Life of Roger Williams.* [NH 1945]

Religious life—Fiction
Rylant, Cynthia. *A Fine White Dust.* [NH 1987]

Responsibility—Fiction
Carlson, Natalie Savage. *The Family under the Bridge.* [NH 1959]

Engdahl, Sylvia Louise. *Enchantress from the Stars.* [NH 1971]

Rhoads, Dorothy. *The Corn Grows Ripe.* [NH 1957]

Revenge—Fiction
Speare, Elizabeth George. *The Bronze Bow.* [NA 1962]

Revolutionaries—18th century—Biography
Gurko, Leo. *Tom Paine, Freedom's Apostle.* [NH 1958]

Rice—Fiction
Treffinger, Carolyn. *Li Lun, Lad of Courage.* [NH 1948]

Rifles—Fiction
Fox, Paula. *One-Eyed Cat.* [NH 1985]

Hewes, Agnes Danforth. *The Codfish Musket.* [NH 1937]

Riots—California—Los Angeles—Fiction
Bunting, Eve. *Smoky Night.* Illus. by David Diaz. [CA 1995]

River life—Ohio River—Fiction
Crawford, Phyllis. *"Hello, the Boat!"* [NH 1939]

Rivers—Fiction
Crawford, Phyllis. *"Hello, the Boat!"* [NH 1939]

Flack, Marjorie. *Boats on the River.* Illus. by Jay Hyde Barnum. [CH 1947]

Holling, Holling C. *Minn of the Mississippi.* [NH 1952]

Meigs, Cornelia. *Swift Rivers.* [NH 1933]

Rawlings, Marjorie Kinnan. *The Secret River.* [NH 1956]

Robbers and outlaws—Fiction
Fleischman, Sid. *The Whipping Boy.* [NA 1987]

Turner, Megan Whalen. *The Thief.* [NH 1997]

Robbers and outlaws—Folklore
Hogrogian, Nonny. *The Contest.* [CH 1977]

Plume, Ilse. *The Bremen-Town Musicians.* Adapted from the Brothers Grimm. [CH 1981]

Robin Hood (Legendary character)
Malcolmson, Anne, editor. *Song of Robin Hood.* Illus. by Virginia Lee Burton. [CH 1948]

Roland, Mme (Marie-Jeanne), 1754–1793
Eaton, Jeanette. *A Daughter of the Seine: The Life of Madame Roland.* [NH 1930]

Roller skating—Fiction
Sawyer, Ruth. *Roller Skates.* [NA 1937]

Rome—History—Empire, 30 B.C.–284 A.D.—Fiction
Snedeker, Caroline Dale. *The Forgotten Daughter.* [NH 1934]

Speare, Elizabeth George. *The Bronze Bow.* [NA 1962]

Roosevelt, Eleanor, 1884–1962
Freedman, Russell. *Eleanor Roosevelt: A Life of Discovery.* [NH 1994]

Roosevelt, Theodore, 1858–1919
Judson, Clara Ingram. *Theodore Roosevelt, Fighting Patriot.* [NH 1954]

Roosters—Fiction
Cooney, Barbara. *Chanticleer and the Fox.* Text adapted from *Canterbury Tales.* [CA 1959]

Rumpelstiltskin (Folk tale)—Adaptations
Ness, Evaline. *Tom Tit Tot: An English Folk Tale.* [CH 1966]

Zemach, Harve. *Duffy and the Devil: A Cornish Tale.* Illus. by Margot Zemach. [CA 1974]

Runaways—Fiction
Curtis, Christopher Paul. *Bud, Not Buddy.* [NA 2000]

Konigsburg, E. L. *From the Mixed-Up Files of Mrs. Basil E. Frankweiler.* [NA 1968]

Russia—Folklore
Artzybasheff, Boris. *Seven Simeons: A Russian Tale.* [CH 1938]

Ransome, Arthur. *The Fool of the World and the Flying Ship*. Illus. by Uri Shulevitz. **[CA 1969]**

Reyher, Becky. *My Mother is the Most Beautiful Woman in the World*. Illus. by Ruth Chrisman Gannett. **[CH 1946]**

Robbins, Ruth. *Baboushka and the Three Kings*. Illus. by Nicolas Sidjakov. **[CA 1961]**

S

Safety—Fiction

Rathmann, Peggy. *Officer Buckle and Gloria*. **[CA 1996]**

Sailboats—Fiction

Creech, Sharon. *The Wanderer*. **[NH 2001]**

Sailing—Fiction

Brown, Marcia. *Skipper John's Cook*. **[CH 1952]**

Creech, Sharon. *The Wanderer*. **[NH 2001]**

Hawes, Charles. *The Dark Frigate*. **[NA 1924]**

Latham, Jean Lee. *Carry On, Mr. Bowditch*. **[NA 1956]**

Meigs, Cornelia. *Clearing Weather*. **[NH 1929]**

Saint Helens, Mount (Wash.)—Eruption, 1980

Lauber, Patricia. *Volcano: The Eruption and Healing of Mount St. Helens*. **[NH 1987]**

Saint Joseph's Day—California—Fiction

Politi, Leo. *Song of the Swallows*. **[CA 1950]**

San Francisco (Calif.)—Fiction

Freeman, Don. *Fly High, Fly Low*. **[CH 1958]**

Yep, Laurence. *Dragonwings*. **[NH 1976]**

San Joaquin Valley (Calif.)—Fiction

Gates, Doris. *Blue Willow*. **[NH 1941]**

Santa Claus—Fiction

Van Allsburg, Chris. *The Polar Express*. **[CA 1986]**

Saving and investment—Fiction

Williams, Vera B. *A Chair for My Mother*. **[CH 1983]**

Scandinavia—Fiction

Burglon, Nora. *Children of the Soil: A Story of Scandinavia*. **[NH 1933]**

Schools—Fiction

Avi. *Nothing but the Truth: A Documentary Novel*. **[NH 1992]**

Caudill, Rebecca. *A Pocketful of Cricket*. Illus. by Evaline Ness. **[CH 1965]**

Cleary, Beverly. *Dear Mr. Henshaw*. **[NA 1984]**

Cleary, Beverly. *Ramona Quimby, Age 8*. **[NH 1982]**

DeJong, Meindert. *The Wheel on the School*. **[NA 1955]**

Konigsburg, E. L. *The View from Saturday*. **[NA 1997]**

Rathmann, Peggy. *Officer Buckle and Gloria*. **[CA 1996]**

Yashima, Taro. *Crow Boy*. **[CH 1956]**

Science—History

Shippen, Katherine B. *Men, Microscopes, and Living Things*. **[NH 1956]**

Science fiction

Farmer, Nancy. *The Ear, the Eye, and the Arm.* [NH 1995]

Farmer, Nancy. *The House of the Scorpion.* [NH 2003]

L'Engle, Madeleine. *A Wrinkle in Time.* [NA 1963]

Lowry, Lois. *The Giver.* [NA 1994]

Scientists—Biography

Martin, Jacqueline Briggs. *Snowflake Bentley.* Illus. by Mary Azarian. [CA 1999]

Shippen, Katherine B. *Men, Microscopes, and Living Things.* [NH 1956]

Sís, Peter. *Starry Messenger: A Book Depicting the Life of a Famous Scientist, Mathematician, Astronomer, Philosopher, Physicist, Galileo Galilei.* [CH 1997]

Scotland—Fiction

Leaf, Munro. *Wee Gillis.* Illus. by Robert Lawson. [CH 1939]

Scotland—Folklore

Leodhas, Sorche Nic, pseud. (Leclaire Alger). *All in the Morning Early.* Illus. by Evaline Ness. [CH 1964]

Leodhas, Sorche Nic, pseud. (Leclaire Alger). *Thistle and Thyme: Tales and Legends from Scotland.* [NH 1963]

Young, Ella. *The Tangle-Coated Horse and Other Tales.* [NH 1930]

Scotland—History—1057–1603—Fiction

de Angeli, Marguerite. *Black Fox of Lorne.* [NH 1957]

Scotland—History—18th century—Fiction

Gray, Elizabeth Janet (Elizabeth Gray Vining). *Young Walter Scott.* [NH 1936]

Scotland—Songs and music

Leodhas, Sorche Nic, pseud. (Leclaire Alger). *Always Room for One More.* Illus. by Nonny Hogrogian. [CA 1966]

Scott, Walter, Sir, 1771–1832—Fiction

Gray, Elizabeth Janet (Elizabeth Gray Vining). *Young Walter Scott.* [NH 1936]

Sea lions—Fiction

Schreiber, Georges. *Bambino the Clown.* [CH 1948]

Sea stories

Avi. *The True Confessions of Charlotte Doyle.* [NH 1991]

Colum, Padraic. *The Voyagers: Being Legends and Romances of Atlantic Discovery.* [NH 1926]

Creech, Sharon. *The Wanderer.* [NH 2001]

Fox, Paula. *The Slave Dancer.* [NA 1974]

Hawes, Charles. *The Dark Frigate.* [NA 1924]

Hawes, Charles. *The Great Quest.* [NH 1922]

Hewes, Agnes Danforth. *Glory of the Seas.* [NH 1934]

Holling, Holling C. *Seabird.* [NH 1949]

Lofting, Hugh. *The Voyages of Doctor Dolittle.* [NA 1923]

Sperry, Armstrong. *All Sail Set: A Romance of the Flying Cloud.* [NH 1936]

Tietjens, Eunice. *Boy of the South Seas*. [NH 1932]

Seals (Animals)—Fiction

Schreiber, Georges. *Bambino the Clown*. [CH 1948]

Seashore animals

Goudey, Alice E. *Houses from the Sea*. Illus. by Adrienne Adams. [CH 1960]

Seasons—Fiction

Birnbaum, A. *Green Eyes*. [CH 1954]

Hall, Donald. *Ox-Cart Man*. Illus. by Barbara Cooney. [CA 1980]

MacDonald, Golden, pseud. (Margaret Wise Brown). *The Little Island*. Illus. by Leonard Weisgard. [CA 1947]

Seasons—Poetry

Updike, John. *A Child's Calendar*. Illus. by Trina Schart Hyman. [CH 2000]

Self-reliance—Fiction

Bishop, Claire Huchet. *All Alone*. [NH 1954]

Carlson, Natalie Savage. *The Family under the Bridge*. [NH 1959]

George, Jean Craighead. *My Side of the Mountain*. [NH 1960]

Horvath, Polly. *Everything on a Waffle*. [NH 2002]

McGraw, Eloise Jarvis. *The Golden Goblet*. [NH 1962]

O'Dell, Scott. *Island of the Blue Dolphins*. [NA 1961]

Seneca Indians—Fiction

Lenski, Lois. *Indian Captive: The Story of Mary Jemison*. [NH 1942]

Sex role—Fiction

Avi. *The True Confessions of Charlotte Doyle*. [NH 1991]

Holm, Jennifer L. *Our Only May Amelia*. [NH 2000]

Shadows—Poetry

Cendrars, Blaise. *Shadow*. Illus. and trans. by Marcia Brown. [CA 1983]

Shape

Ehlert, Lois. *Color Zoo*. [CH 1990]

Sharing—Fiction

Newberry, Clare Turlay. *Barkis*. [CH 1939]

Sharing—Folklore

Brown, Marcia. *Stone Soup*. [CH 1948]

Sheep—Fiction

Krumgold, Joseph. *... And Now Miguel*. [NA 1954]

MacDonald, Golden, pseud. (Margaret Wise Brown). *Little Lost Lamb*. Illus. by Leonard Weisgard. [CA 1946]

Yates, Elizabeth. *Mountain Born*. [NH 1944]

Sheep ranchers—Fiction

Krumgold, Joseph. *... And Now Miguel*. [NA 1954]

Wier, Ester. *The Loner*. [NH 1964]

Shells

Goudey, Alice E. *Houses from the Sea*. Illus. by Adrienne Adams. [CH 1960]

Shepherds—Fiction

Kalashnikoff, Nicholas. *The Defender*. [NH 1952]

Krumgold, Joseph. *... And Now Miguel*. [NA 1954]

MacDonald, Golden, pseud. (Margaret Wise Brown). *Little Lost Lamb*. Illus. by Leonard Weisgard. **[CA 1946]**

Schaefer, Jack. *Old Ramon*. **[NH 1961]**

Yates, Elizabeth. *Mountain Born*. **[NH 1944]**

Ship captains—Fiction

Latham, Jean Lee. *Carry On, Mr. Bowditch*. **[NA 1956]**

Shipbuilding—Fiction

Meigs, Cornelia. *Clearing Weather*. **[NH 1929]**

Shipping—History

Holling, Holling C. *Seabird*. **[NH 1949]**

Ships—Fiction

Flack, Marjorie. *Boats on the River*. Illus. by Jay Hyde Barnum. **[CH 1947]**

Tietjens, Eunice. *Boy of the South Seas*. **[NH 1932]**

Ships—History

Holling, Holling C. *Seabird*. **[NH 1949]**

Ships—Models—Fiction

Kingman, Lee. *Pierre Pidgeon*. Illus. by Arnold E. Bare. **[CH 1944]**

Shipwrecks—Fiction

de Angeli, Marguerite. *Black Fox of Lorne*. **[NH 1957]**

Parrish, Anne. *Floating Island*. **[NH 1931]**

Shoemakers—Fiction

Ets, Marie Hall. *Mr. T. W. Anthony Woo*. **[CH 1952]**

Shona (African people)—Fiction

Farmer, Nancy. *A Girl Named Disaster*. **[NH 1997]**

Shopping—Fiction

Lobel, Arnold. *On Market Street*. Illus. by Anita Lobel. **[CH 1982]**

Short stories

Bennett, John. *The Pigtail of Ah Lee Ben Loo*. **[NA 1927]**

Brittain, Bill and Andrew Glass. *The Wish Giver: Three Tales of Coven Tree*. **[NH 1984]**

Fleischman, Paul and Andrew Glass. *Graven Images*. **[NH 1983]**

McKissack, Patricia. *The Dark-Thirty: Southern Tales of the Supernatural*. **[NH 1993]**

Scieszka, Jon. *The Stinky Cheese Man and Other Fairly Stupid Tales*. Illus. by Lane Smith. **[CH 1993]**

Short stories, African

Courlander, Harold. *The Cow-Tail Switch, and Other West African Stories*. **[NH 1948]**

Short stories, Chinese

Chrisman, Arthur Bowie. *Shen of the Sea*. **[NA 1926]**

Short stories, Mediterranean

Hallock, Grace. *The Boy Who Was*. **[NH 1929]**

Siberia (Russia)—Fiction

Kalashnikoff, Nicholas. *The Defender*. **[NH 1952]**

Lide, Alice Alison. *Ood-le-uk the Wanderer*. **[NH 1931]**

Sick—Fiction

Bemelmans, Ludwig. *Madeline*. **[CH 1940]**

Thurber, James. *Many Moons.* Illus. by Louis Slobodkin. **[CA 1944]**

Siegal, Aranka—Childhood and youth

Siegal, Aranka. *Upon the Head of the Goat: A Childhood in Hungary, 1939–1944.* **[NH 1982]**

Sierra Nevada (Calif. and Nev.)—Fiction

Yep, Laurence. *Dragon's Gate.* **[NH 1994]**

Single-parent family—Fiction

Coman, Carolyn. *What Jamie Saw.* **[NH 1996]**

Hamilton, Virginia. *Sweet Whispers, Brother Rush.* **[NH 1983]**

Voigt, Cynthia. *A Solitary Blue.* **[NH 1984]**

Sisters—Fiction

Couloumbis, Audrey. *Getting Near to Baby.* **[NH 2000]**

Goudey, Alice E. *The Day We Saw the Sun Come Up.* Illus. by Adrienne Adams. **[CH 1962]**

Paterson, Katherine. *Jacob Have I Loved.* **[NA 1981]**

Sendak, Maurice. *Outside Over There.* **[CH 1982]**

Sisters—Folklore

San Souci, Robert D. *The Talking Eggs: A Folktale from the American South.* Illus. by Jerry Pinkney. **[CH 1990]**

Steptoe, John. *Mufaro's Beautiful Daughters: An African Tale.* **[CH 1988]**

Young, Ed. *Lon Po Po: A Red-Riding Hood Story from China.* **[CA 1990]**

Skunks—Fiction

Montgomery, Rutherford. *Kildee House.* **[NH 1950]**

Slave trade

Bontemps, Arna. *Story of the Negro.* **[NH 1949]**

Slave trade—Fiction

Fox, Paula. *The Slave Dancer.* **[NA 1974]**

Hawes, Charles. *The Great Quest.* **[NH 1922]**

Singmaster, Elsie. *Swords of Steel: The Story of a Gettysburg Boy.* **[NH 1934]**

Slavery—History

Bontemps, Arna. *Story of the Negro.* **[NH 1949]**

Slavery—Rome—Fiction

Snedeker, Caroline Dale. *The Forgotten Daughter.* **[NH 1934]**

Slavery—United States—Fiction

Swift, Hildegarde Hoyt. *The Railroad to Freedom: A Story of the Civil War.* **[NH 1933]**

Slavery—United States—History

Lester, Julius. *To Be a Slave.* **[NH 1969]**

Slaves—Massachusetts—Biography

Yates, Elizabeth. *Amos Fortune, Free Man.* **[NA 1951]**

Sleep—Fiction

Brown, Margaret Wise. *A Child's Good Night Book.* Illus. by Jean Charlot. **[CH 1944]**

Sleep—Poetry

Ho, Minfong. *Hush! A Thai Lullaby.* Illus. by Holly Meade. **[CH 1997]**

Smoking—Fiction
Cleary, Beverly. *Ramona and Her Father.* [NH 1978]

Snapping turtles—Fiction
Holling, Holling C. *Minn of the Mississippi.* [NH 1952]

Snow—Fiction
Hader, Berta & Elmer. *The Big Snow.* [CA 1949]

Keats, Ezra Jack. *The Snowy Day.* [CA 1963]

Krauss, Ruth. *The Happy Day.* Illus. by Marc Simont. [CH 1950]

Shulevitz, Uri. *Snow.* [CH 1999]

Tresselt, Alvin. *White Snow, Bright Snow.* Illus. by Roger Duvoisin. [CA 1948]

Snowflakes
Martin, Jacqueline Briggs. *Snowflake Bentley.* Illus. by Mary Azarian. [CA 1999]

Soldiers—Fiction
Andersen, H. C. (Hans Christian). *The Steadfast Tin Soldier.* Illus. by Marcia Brown; trans. by M. R. James. [CH 1954]

DeJong, Meindert. *The House of Sixty Fathers.* [NH 1957]

Emberley, Barbara. *Drummer Hoff.* Illus. by Ed Emberley. [CA 1968]

Keith, Harold. *Rifles for Watie.* [NA 1958]

Soldiers—France—Folklore
Brown, Marcia. *Stone Soup.* [CH 1948]

Soldiers—United States—Biography
Holbrook, Stewart. *America's Ethan Allen.* Illus. by Lynd Ward. [CH 1950]

Songs
Politi, Leo. *Juanita.* [CH 1949]

Politi, Leo. *Pedro, the Angel of Olvera Street.* [CH 1947]

Politi, Leo. *Song of the Swallows.* [CA 1950]

Spier, Peter. *Fox Went Out on a Chilly Night: An Old Song.* [CH 1962]

Wheeler, Opal. *Sing Mother Goose.* Illus. by Marjorie Torrey. [CH 1946]

South America—Fiction
Armer, Laura Adams. *The Forest Pool.* [CH 1939]

South America—Folklore
Finger, Charles. *Tales from Silver Lands.* [NA 1925]

South Dakota—Fiction
McNeely, Marian Hurd. *The Jumping-Off Place.* [NH 1930]

Wilder, Laura Ingalls. *By the Shores of Silver Lake.* [NH 1940]

Wilder, Laura Ingalls. *Little Town on the Prairie.* [NH 1942]

Wilder, Laura Ingalls. *The Long Winter.* [NH 1941]

Wilder, Laura Ingalls. *These Happy Golden Years.* [NH 1944]

Southern States—Fiction
McKissack, Patricia. *The Dark-Thirty: Southern Tales of the Supernatural.* [NH 1993]

Southern States—Folklore
San Souci, Robert D. *The Talking Eggs: A Folktale from the American South.* Illus. by Jerry Pinkney. [CH 1990]

Space and time—Fiction
Engdahl, Sylvia Louise. *Enchantress from the Stars.* [NH 1971]

L'Engle, Madeleine. *A Wrinkle in Time*. **[NA 1963]**

Spain—Fiction
Wojciechowska, Maia. *Shadow of a Bull*. **[NA 1965]**

Spain—History—Fiction
Trevino, Elizabeth Borton de. *I, Juan de Pareja*. **[NA 1966]**

Spanish—American War, 1898
Judson, Clara Ingram. *Theodore Roosevelt, Fighting Patriot*. **[NH 1954]**

Spiders—Fiction
Jukes, Mavis. *Like Jake and Me*. **[NH 1985]**
White, E. B. *Charlotte's Web*. **[NH 1952]**

Spiders—Poetry
Howitt, Mary. *The Spider and the Fly*. Illus. by Tony DiTerlizzi. **[CH 2003]**

Spies—Fiction
Fisher, Cyrus, pseud. (Darwin L. Teilhet). *The Avion My Uncle Flew*. **[NH 1947]**
Keith, Harold. *Rifles for Watie*. **[NA 1958]**

Spring—Fiction
Krauss, Ruth. *The Happy Day*. Illus. by Marc Simont. **[CH 1950]**

Star-spangled banner (Song)—Fiction
Avi. *Nothing but the Truth: A Documentary Novel*. **[NH 1992]**

Statesmen—India—Biography
Eaton, Jeanette. *Gandhi, Fighter without a Sword*. **[NH 1951]**

Statesmen—Norway—Biography
Hall, Anna Gertrude. *Nansen*. **[NH 1941]**

Statesmen—United States—Biography
Rourke, Constance. *Davy Crockett*. **[NH 1935]**

Statues—Fiction
Fleischman, Paul and Andrew Glass. *Graven Images*. **[NH 1983]**
Konigsburg, E. L. *From the Mixed-Up Files of Mrs. Basil E. Frankweiler*. **[NA 1968]**

Stepchildren—Fiction
Snyder, Zilpha Keatley. *The Headless Cupid*. **[NH 1972]**

Stepfamilies—Fiction
Blos, Joan W. *A Gathering of Days: A New England Girl's Journal, 1830–1832*. **[NA 1980]**
Brooks, Bruce. *What Hearts*. **[NH 1993]**
Jukes, Mavis. *Like Jake and Me*. **[NH 1985]**
Kalashnikoff, Nicholas. *The Defender*. **[NH 1952]**
MacLachlan, Patricia. *Sarah, Plain and Tall*. **[NA 1986]**

Stepfamilies—Folklore
Brown, Marcia. *Cinderella, or the Little Glass Slipper*. Adapted from Charles Perrault. **[CA 1955]**

Stepmothers—Folklore
Gág, Wanda. *Snow White and the Seven Dwarfs*. Adapted from the Brothers Grimm. **[CH 1939]**

Jarrell, Randall. *Snow-White and the Seven Dwarfs*. Illus. by Nancy Ekholm Burkert; adapted from the Brothers Grimm. **[CH 1973]**

Stores, Retail—Fiction

Crawford, Phyllis. *"Hello, the Boat!"* **[NH 1939]**

Stories in rhyme

Bemelmans, Ludwig. *Madeline*. **[CH 1940]**

Bemelmans, Ludwig. *Madeline's Rescue*. **[CA 1954]**

de Regniers, Beatrice Schenk. *May I Bring a Friend?* Illus. by Beni Montresor. **[CA 1965]**

Emberley, Barbara. *Drummer Hoff*. Illus. by Ed Emberley. **[CA 1968]**

Fleming, Denise. *In the Small, Small Pond*. **[CH 1994]**

Gág, Wanda. *The ABC Bunny*. **[NH 1934]**

Graham, Al. *Timothy Turtle*. Illus. by Tony Palazzo. **[CH 1947]**

Ho, Minfong. *Hush! A Thai Lullaby*. Illus. by Holly Meade. **[CH 1997]**

Langstaff, John. *Frog Went-A-Courtin'*. Illus. by Fedor Rojankovsky. **[CA 1956]**

Leodhas, Sorche Nic, pseud. (Leclaire Alger). *All in the Morning Early*. Illus. by Evaline Ness. **[CH 1964]**

Lobel, Arnold. *On Market Street*. Illus. by Anita Lobel. **[CH 1982]**

Moss, Lloyd. *Zin! Zin! Zin! A Violin*. Illus. by Marjorie Priceman. **[CH 1996]**

Preston, Edna Mitchell. *Pop Corn & Ma Goodness*. Illus. by Robert Andrew Parker. **[CH 1970]**

Seuss, Dr., pseud. (Theodor Seuss Geisel). *If I Ran the Zoo*. **[CH 1951]**

Seuss, Dr., pseud. (Theodor Seuss Geisel). *McElligot's Pool*. **[CH 1948]**

Tudor, Tasha. *1 Is One*. **[CH 1957]**

Zemach, Harve. *The Judge: An Untrue Tale*. Illus. by Margot Zemach. **[CH 1970]**

Stories without words

Bang, Molly. *The Grey Lady and the Strawberry Snatcher*. **[CH 1981]**

Crews, Donald. *Truck*. **[CH 1981]**

Rohmann, Eric. *Time Flies*. **[CH 1995]**

Spier, Peter. *Noah's Ark*. **[CA 1978]**

Tafuri, Nancy. *Have You Seen My Duckling?* **[CH 1985]**

Wiesner, David. *Free Fall*. **[CH 1989]**

Wiesner, David. *Sector 7*. **[CH 2000]**

Wiesner, David. *Tuesday*. **[CA 1992]**

Storks—Fiction

Brown, Margaret Wise. *Wheel on the Chimney*. Illus. by Tibor Gergely. **[CH 1955]**

DeJong, Meindert. *The Wheel on the School*. **[NA 1955]**

Storms—Fiction

Zolotow, Charlotte. *The Storm Book*. Illus. by Margaret Bloy Graham. **[CH 1953]**

Storytelling—Fiction

Paulsen, Gary. *The Winter Room*. **[NH 1990]**

Storytelling—Folklore

Haley, Gail E. *A Story A Story: An African Tale*. **[CA 1971]**

Strawberries—Fiction

Bang, Molly. *The Grey Lady and the Strawberry Snatcher*. **[CH 1981]**

Lenski, Lois. *Strawberry Girl.*
[NA 1946]

Summer—Fiction

Allee, Marjorie Hill. *Jane's Island.*
[NH 1932]

Byars, Betsy. *Summer of the Swans.*
[NA 1971]

Enright, Elizabeth. *Gone-Away Lake.*
[NH 1958]

Enright, Elizabeth. *Thimble Summer.*
[NA 1939]

McCloskey, Robert. *Time of Wonder.*
[CA 1958]

Sun—Fiction

Goudey, Alice E. *The Day We Saw the Sun Come Up.* Illus. by Adrienne Adams. [CH 1962]

Sun—Folklore

Baylor, Byrd. *The Way to Start a Day.* Illus. by Peter Parnall.
[CH 1979]

Belting, Natalia M. *The Sun Is a Golden Earring.* Illus. by Bernarda Bryson. [CH 1963]

Dayrell, Elphinstone. *Why the Sun and the Moon Live in the Sky: A Nigerian Tale.* Illus. by Blair Lent.
[CH 1969]

McDermott, Gerald. *Raven: A Trickster Tale from the Pacific Northwest.*
[CH 1994]

Supernatural—Fiction

Farmer, Nancy. *A Girl Named Disaster.*
[NH 1997]

Maxwell, William. *The Heavenly Tenants.* [NH 1947]

McKissack, Patricia. *The Dark-Thirty: Southern Tales of the Supernatural.*
[NH 1993]

Supernatural—Folklore

San Souci, Robert D. *The Faithful Friend.* Illus. by Brian Pinkney.
[CH 1996]

Survival—Fiction

Eckert, Allan W. *Incident at Hawk's Hill.* [NH 1972]

Farmer, Nancy. *A Girl Named Disaster.*
[NH 1997]

Fleischman, Sid. *The Whipping Boy.*
[NA 1987]

George, Jean Craighead. *Julie of the Wolves.* [NA 1973]

George, Jean Craighead. *My Side of the Mountain.* [NH 1960]

McGraw, Eloise Jarvis. *Moccasin Trail.*
[NH 1953]

O'Dell, Scott. *Island of the Blue Dolphins.* [NA 1961]

Paulsen, Gary. *Hatchet.* [NH 1988]

Speare, Elizabeth George. *The Sign of the Beaver.* [NH 1984]

Sperry, Armstrong. *Call It Courage.*
[NA 1941]

Steig, William. *Abel's Island.*
[NH 1977]

Swahili language

Feelings, Muriel. *Jambo Means Hello: Swahili Alphabet Book.* Illus. by Tom Feelings. [CH 1975]

Feelings, Muriel. *Moja Means One: Swahili Counting Book.* Illus. by Tom Feelings. [CH 1972]

Swallows—Fiction

Politi, Leo. *Song of the Swallows.*
[CA 1950]

Swans—Fiction

Pinkney, Jerry. *The Ugly Duckling.* Adapted from Hans Christian Andersen. [CH 2000]

Sweden—Fiction
Burglon, Nora. *Children of the Soil: A Story of Scandinavia.* [NH 1933]

Swedish Americans—Fiction
Lindquist, Jennie. *The Golden Name Day.* [NH 1956]

Switzerland—Fiction
Buff, Mary & Conrad. *The Apple and the Arrow.* [NH 1952]

Switzerland—History—Fiction
Davis, Julia. *Mountains Are Free.* [NH 1931]

Synagogues—Fiction
Kimmel, Eric. *Hershel and the Hanukkah Goblins.* Illus. by Trina Schart Hyman. [CH 1990]

T

Taliesin—Fiction
Bond, Nancy. *A String in the Harp.* [NH 1977]

Tall tales
Issacs, Anne. *Swamp Angel.* Illus. by Paul O. Zelinsky. [CH 1995]

Lester, Julius. *John Henry.* Illus. by Jerry Pinkney. [CH 1995]

Teacher-student relationships—Fiction
Caudill, Rebecca. *A Pocketful of Cricket.* Illus. by Evaline Ness. [CH 1965]

Konigsburg, E. L. *The View from Saturday.* [NA 1997]

Yashima, Taro. *Crow Boy.* [CH 1956]

Teachers—Fiction
Wilder, Laura Ingalls. *These Happy Golden Years.* [NH 1944]

Teaching—Fiction
Dalgliesh, Alice. *The Silver Pencil.* [NH 1945]

Teasing—Fiction
Hader, Berta & Elmer. *Cock-a-Doodle Doo.* [CH 1940]

Teeth—Fiction
McCloskey, Robert. *One Morning in Maine.* [CH 1953]

Tell, William (Legendary character)
Buff, Mary & Conrad. *The Apple and the Arrow.* [NH 1952]

Davis, Julia. *Mountains Are Free.* [NH 1931]

Temper—Fiction
Bang, Molly. *When Sophie Gets Angry—Really, Really Angry.* [CH 2000]

Tennessee—Fiction
Issacs, Anne. *Swamp Angel.* Illus. by Paul O. Zelinsky. [CH 1995]

Terminally ill—Fiction
Ish-Kishor, Sulamith. *Our Eddie.* [NH 1970]

L'Engle, Madeleine. *A Ring of Endless Light.* [NH 1981]

Tewa Indians—Social life and customs
Clark, Ann Nolan. *In My Mother's House.* Illus. by Velino Herrera. [CH 1942]

Thailand—Poetry
Ho, Minfong. *Hush! A Thai Lullaby.* Illus. by Holly Meade. [CH 1997]

Thanksgiving Day—Fiction
Dalgliesh, Alice. *The Thanksgiving Story.* Illus. by Helen Sewell. [CH 1955]

Theater—Fiction
Tolan, Stephanie S. *Surviving the Applewhites.* [NH 2003]

Thumb, Tom, 1838–1883
Hunt, Mabel Leigh. *"Have You Seen Tom Thumb?"* [NH 1943]

Tibet (China)—Description and travel
Sís, Peter. *Tibet: Through the Red Box.* [CH 1999]

Tibet (China)—Fiction
Rankin, Louise. *Daughter of the Mountains.* [NH 1949]

Tigers—Fiction
Stolz, Mary. *Belling the Tiger.* [NH 1962]

Tightrope walking—Fiction
McCully, Emily Arnold. *Mirette on the High Wire.* [CA 1993]

Time travel—Fiction
Bond, Nancy. *A String in the Harp.* [NH 1977]

Cooper, Susan. *The Dark Is Rising.* [NH 1974]

Rohmann, Eric. *Time Flies.* [CH 1995]

Tlingit Indians—Folklore
Sleator, William. *The Angry Moon.* Illus. by Blair Lent. [CH 1971]

Toads—Fiction
Lobel, Arnold. *Frog and Toad Are Friends.* [CH 1971]

Lobel, Arnold. *Frog and Toad Together.* [NH 1973]

Tobacco—Fiction
Bowen, William. *The Old Tobacco Shop.* [NH 1922]

Tohono O'Odham Indians
Baylor, Byrd. *The Desert Is Theirs.* Illus. by Peter Parnall. [CH 1976]

Toy and movable books
Taback, Simms. *Joseph Had a Little Overcoat.* [CA 2000]

Taback, Simms. *There Was an Old Lady Who Swallowed a Fly.* [CH 1998]

Toys—Fiction
Andersen, H. C. (Hans Christian). *The Steadfast Tin Soldier.* Illus. by Marcia Brown; trans. by M. R. James. [CH 1954]

Lionni, Leo. *Alexander and the Wind-Up Mouse.* [CH 1970]

Tramps—Fiction
Carlson, Natalie Savage. *The Family under the Bridge.* [NH 1959]

Travelers—Fiction
Besterman, Catherine. *The Quaint and Curious Quest of Johnny Longfoot.* [NH 1948]

McGraw, Eloise Jarvis. *Moccasin Trail.* [NH 1953]

Meader, Stephen W. *Boy with a Pack.* [NH 1940]

Rankin, Louise. *Daughter of the Mountains.* [NH 1949]

Gray, Elizabeth Janet (Elizabeth Gray Vining). *Adam of the Road.* [NA 1943]

Treasure hunts—Folklore
Shulevitz, Uri. *The Treasure.* [CH 1980]

Trees
Udry, Janice May. *A Tree Is Nice.* Illus. by Marc Simont. [CA 1957]

Trees—Fiction
Buff, Mary & Conrad. *Big Tree.* [NH 1947]

Tricks—Fiction
Kepes, Juliet. *Five Little Monkeys.* [CH 1953]

Tricksters—Folklore
McDermott, Gerald. *Raven: A Trickster Tale from the Pacific Northwest.* [CH 1994]

Stevens, Janet. *Tops & Bottoms.* [CH 1996]

Trinidad and Tobago—Fiction
Dalgliesh, Alice. *The Silver Pencil.* [NH 1945]

Trucks—Fiction
Crews, Donald. *Truck.* [CH 1981]

Trumpet—Fiction
Isadora, Rachel. *Ben's Trumpet.* [CH 1980]

Tsunamis—Folklore
Hodges, Margaret. *The Wave.* Illus. by Blair Lent. [CH 1965]

Tubman, Harriet, 1820-1913—Fiction
Swift, Hildegarde Hoyt. *The Railroad to Freedom: A Story of the Civil War.* [NH 1933]

Turtles—Fiction
Graham, Al. *Timothy Turtle.* Illus. by Tony Palazzo. [CH 1947]

Holling, Holling C. *Minn of the Mississippi.* [NH 1952]

Twins—Fiction
de Angeli, Marguerite. *Black Fox of Lorne.* [NH 1957]

Paterson, Katherine. *Jacob Have I Loved.* [NA 1981]

Van Stockum, Hilda. *A Day on Skates: The Story of a Dutch Picnic.* [NH 1935]

Typewriters—Fiction
Cronin, Doreen. *Click, Clack, Moo: Cows That Type.* Illus. by Betsy Lewin. [CH 2001]

U

Ukraine—Folklore
Reyher, Becky. *My Mother is the Most Beautiful Woman in the World.* Illus. by Ruth Chrisman Gannett. [CH 1946]

Umbrellas and parasols—Fiction
Yashima, Taro. *Umbrella.* [CH 1959]

Uncles—Fiction
Besterman, Catherine. *The Quaint and Curious Quest of Johnny Longfoot.* [NH 1948]

Fisher, Cyrus, pseud. (Darwin L. Teilhet). *The Avion My Uncle Flew.* [NH 1947]

Horvath, Polly. *Everything on a Waffle.* [NH 2002]

Martin, Ann M. *A Corner of the Universe.* [NH 2003]

Paulsen, Gary. *The Winter Room.* [NH 1990]

Stewart, Sarah. *The Gardener.* Illus. by David Small. [CH 1998]

Underground railroad—Fiction
Swift, Hildegarde Hoyt. *The Railroad to Freedom: A Story of the Civil War.* [NH 1933]

Unemployment—Fiction

Cleary, Beverly. *Ramona and Her Father.* [NH 1978]

United States—Description and travel—Fiction

Creech, Sharon. *Walk Two Moons.* [NA 1995]

Say, Allen. *Grandfather's Journey.* [CA 1994]

United States—Emigration and immigration—Fiction

Lawson, Robert. *The Great Wheel.* [NH 1958]

United States—Folklore

Lester, Julius. *John Henry.* Illus. by Jerry Pinkney. [CH 1995]

Sawyer, Ruth. *Journey Cake, Ho!* Illus. by Robert McCloskey. [CH 1954]

Stevens, Janet. *Tops & Bottoms.* [CH 1996]

United States—Foreign relations—Japan

Blumberg, Rhoda. *Commodore Perry in the Land of the Shogun.* [NH 1986]

United States—History

Tunis, Edwin. *Frontier Living.* [NH 1962]

United States—History—Civil War, 1861–1865

Freedman, Russell. *Lincoln: A Photobiography.* [NA 1988]

Judson, Clara Ingram. *Abraham Lincoln, Friend of the People.* [NH 1951]

United States—History—Civil War, 1861–1865—Fiction

Hunt, Irene. *Across Five Aprils.* [NH 1965]

Keith, Harold. *Rifles for Watie.* [NA 1958]

Singmaster, Elsie. *Swords of Steel: The Story of a Gettysburg Boy.* [NH 1934]

Steele, William O. *The Perilous Road.* [NH 1959]

Swift, Hildegarde Hoyt. *The Railroad to Freedom: A Story of the Civil War.* [NH 1933]

United States—History—Colonial period, ca. 1600–1775

Foster, Genevieve. *George Washington.* [NH 1950]

Johnson, Gerald W. *America Is Born: A History for Peter.* [NH 1960]

United States—History—French and Indian War, 1755–1763—Fiction

Edmonds, Walter Dumaux. *The Matchlock Gun.* [NA 1942]

United States—History—Miscellanea

Petersham, Maud & Miska. *An American ABC.* [CH 1942]

United States—History—19th century

Foster, Genevieve. *Abraham Lincoln's World.* [NH 1945]

United States—History—Revolution, 1775–1783

Holbrook, Stewart. *America's Ethan Allen.* Illus. by Lynd Ward. [CH 1950]

United States—History—Revolution, 1775–1783—Fiction

Caudill, Rebecca. *Tree of Freedom.* [NH 1950]

Collier, James Lincoln & Christopher. *My Brother Sam Is Dead.* [NH 1975]

Forbes, Esther. *Johnny Tremain.* [NA 1944]

United States—History—Revolution, 1775–1783—Participation, Female—Fiction

Gray, Elizabeth Janet (Elizabeth Gray Vining). *Meggy MacIntosh.* [NH 1931]

United States—History—20th century

Johnson, Gerald W. *America Moves Forward: A History for Peter.* [NH 1961]

United States—Social life and customs

Tunis, Edwin. *Frontier Living.* [NH 1962]

United States—Social life and customs—20th century—Fiction

Rylant, Cynthia. *When I Was Young in the Mountains.* Illus. by Diane Goode. [CH 1983]

United States—Songs and music

Emberley, Barbara. *One Wide River to Cross.* Illus. by Ed Emberley. [CH 1967]

United States—Supreme Court—Biography

Judson, Clara Ingram. *Mr. Justice Holmes.* [NH 1957]

United States Naval Expedition to Japan, 1852–1854

Blumberg, Rhoda. *Commodore Perry in the Land of the Shogun.* [NH 1986]

United States—Congress—House—Biography

Rourke, Constance. *Davy Crockett.* [NH 1935]

Universe—Folklore

Belting, Natalia M. *The Sun Is a Golden Earring.* Illus. by Bernarda Bryson. [CH 1963]

V

Vacations—Fiction

Enright, Elizabeth. *Gone-Away Lake.* [NH 1958]

Vaudeville—Fiction

Ackerman, Karen. *Song and Dance Man.* Illus. by Stephen Gammell. [CA 1989]

Velázquez, Diego, 1599–1660—Fiction

Trevino, Elizabeth Borton de. *I, Juan de Pareja.* [NA 1966]

Vermont—Fiction

Coblentz, Catherine. *The Blue Cat of Castle Town.* [NH 1950]

Vermont—History—Revolution, 1775–1783

Holbrook, Stewart. *America's Ethan Allen.* Illus. by Lynd Ward. [CH 1950]

Vikings—Fiction

de Angeli, Marguerite. *Black Fox of Lorne.* [NH 1957]

Villages—Fiction

DeJong, Meindert. *The Wheel on the School.* [NA 1955]

Kendall, Carol. *The Gammage Cup.* [NH 1960]

Sauer, Julia. *Fog Magic*. **[NH 1944]**

Violence—Fiction
Spinelli, Jerry. *Wringer*. **[NH 1998]**

Virgin Islands—Fiction
Brown, Marcia. *Henry Fisherman*. **[CH 1950]**

Virginia—Fiction
Paterson, Katherine. *Bridge to Terabithia*. **[NA 1978]**

White, Ruth. *Belle Prater's Boy*. **[NH 1997]**

Volcanoes
Lauber, Patricia. *Volcano: The Eruption and Healing of Mount St. Helens*. **[NH 1987]**

Voyages and travels—Fiction
Besterman, Catherine. *The Quaint and Curious Quest of Johnny Longfoot*. **[NH 1948]**

Creech, Sharon. *Walk Two Moons*. **[NA 1995]**

Creech, Sharon. *The Wanderer*. **[NH 2001]**

du Bois, William Pène. *The Twenty-One Balloons*. **[NA 1948]**

Holling, Holling C. *Paddle-to-the-Sea*. **[CH 1942]**

Holling, Holling C. *Seabird*. **[NH 1949]**

Maxwell, William. *The Heavenly Tenants*. **[NH 1947]**

Rankin, Louise. *Daughter of the Mountains*. **[NH 1949]**

Say, Allen. *Grandfather's Journey*. **[CA 1994]**

Sís, Peter. *Tibet: Through the Red Box*. **[CH 1999]**

W

Wales—Fiction
Bond, Nancy. *A String in the Harp*. **[NH 1977]**

Cooper, Susan. *The Grey King*. **[NA 1976]**

Jones, Idwal. *Whistler's Van*. **[NH 1937]**

Walt Disney Company—Biography
Peet, Bill. *Bill Peet: An Autobiography*. **[CH 1990]**

Washington (State)—Fiction
Holm, Jennifer L. *Our Only May Amelia*. **[NH 2000]**

Washington, George, 1732–1799
Eaton, Jeanette. *Leader by Destiny: George Washington, Man and Patriot*. **[NH 1939]**

Foster, Genevieve. *George Washington*. **[NH 1950]**

Foster, Genevieve. *George Washington's World*. **[NH 1942]**

Watie, Stand, 1806–1871—Fiction
Keith, Harold. *Rifles for Watie*. **[NA 1958]**

Wealth—Folklore
Brown, Marcia. *Dick Whittington and His Cat*. **[CH 1951]**

Weather—Fiction
McCloskey, Robert. *Time of Wonder*. **[CA 1958]**

Seuss, Dr., pseud. (Theodor Seuss Geisel). *Bartholomew and the Oobleck*. **[CH 1950]**

Tresselt, Alvin. *Rain Drop Splash.* Illus. by Leonard Weisgard. [CH 1947]

West Indies—Folklore

San Souci, Robert D. *The Faithful Friend.* Illus. by Brian Pinkney. [CH 1996]

West (U.S.)—Discovery and exploration

Tunis, Edwin. *Frontier Living.* [NH 1962]

West (U.S.)—Fiction

James, Will. *Smoky, the Cowhorse.* [NA 1927]

McGraw, Eloise Jarvis. *Moccasin Trail.* [NH 1953]

West Virginia—Fiction

Byars, Betsy. *Summer of the Swans.* [NA 1971]

Naylor, Phyllis Reynolds. *Shiloh.* [NA 1992]

Rylant, Cynthia. *Missing May.* [NA 1993]

Rylant, Cynthia. *The Relatives Came.* Illus. by Stephen Gammell. [CH 1986]

Rylant, Cynthia. *When I Was Young in the Mountains.* Illus. by Diane Goode. [CH 1983]

Whittington, Richard, d. 1423—Legends

Brown, Marcia. *Dick Whittington and His Cat.* [CH 1951]

Wild horses—Fiction

Henry, Marguerite. *Misty of Chincoteague.* [NH 1948]

Kalnay, Francis. *Chucaro: Wild Pony of the Pampa.* [NH 1959]

Sandoz, Mari. *The Horsecatcher.* [NH 1958]

Wilder, Laura Ingalls, 1867–1957—Fiction

Wilder, Laura Ingalls. *By the Shores of Silver Lake.* [NH 1940]

Wilder, Laura Ingalls. *Little Town on the Prairie.* [NH 1942]

Wilder, Laura Ingalls. *The Long Winter.* [NH 1941]

Wilder, Laura Ingalls. *On the Banks of Plum Creek.* [NH 1938]

Wilder, Laura Ingalls. *These Happy Golden Years.* [NH 1944]

Wilderness—Fiction

George, Jean Craighead. *My Side of the Mountain.* [NH 1960]

Paulsen, Gary. *Hatchet.* [NH 1988]

Williams, Roger, 1604–1683

Eaton, Jeanette. *Lone Journey: The Life of Roger Williams.* [NH 1945]

Winds—Fiction

McKissack, Patricia C. *Mirandy and Brother Wind.* Illus. by Jerry Pinkney. [CH 1989]

Wiese, Kurt. *Fish in the Air.* [CH 1949]

Winter—Fiction

Bianco, Margery Williams. *Winterbound.* [NH 1937]

Davis, Lavinia R. *Roger and the Fox.* Illus. by Hildegard Woodward. [CH 1948]

Hader, Berta & Elmer. *The Big Snow.* [CA 1949]

Krauss, Ruth. *The Happy Day.* Illus. by Marc Simont. [CH 1950]

Lionni, Leo. *Frederick.* [CH 1968]

Paulsen, Gary. *The Winter Room.* [NH 1990]

Tresselt, Alvin. *White Snow, Bright Snow.* Illus. by Roger Duvoisin. [CA 1948]

Wilder, Laura Ingalls. *The Long Winter.* [NH 1941]

Yolen, Jane. *Owl Moon.* Illus. by John Schoenherr. [CA 1988]

Wisconsin—Biography

North, Sterling. *Rascal: A Memoir of a Better Era.* [NH 1964]

Wisconsin—Fiction

Brink, Carol Ryrie. *Caddie Woodlawn.* [NA 1936]

Enright, Elizabeth. *Thimble Summer.* [NA 1939]

Maxwell, William. *The Heavenly Tenants.* [NH 1947]

Raskin, Ellen. *The Westing Game.* [NA 1979]

Wishes—Fiction

Brittain, Bill and Andrew Glass. *The Wish Giver: Three Tales of Coven Tree.* [NH 1984]

Wit and humor—Fiction

Elkin, Benjamin. *Gillespie and the Guards.* Illus. by James Daugherty. [CH 1957]

Witchcraft—Fiction

Konigsburg, E. L. *Jennifer, Hecate, Macbeth, William McKinley, and Me, Elizabeth.* [NH 1968]

Singer, Isaac Bashevis. *The Fearsome Inn.* [NH 1968]

Snyder, Zilpha Keatley. *The Headless Cupid.* [NH 1972]

Snyder, Zilpha Keatley. *The Witches of Worm.* [NH 1973]

Speare, Elizabeth George. *The Witch of Blackbird Pond.* [NA 1959]

Witches—Folklore

de Paola, Tomie. *Strega Nona: An Old Tale.* [CH 1976]

Gág, Wanda. *Snow White and the Seven Dwarfs.* Adapted from the Brothers Grimm. [CH 1939]

Jarrell, Randall. *Snow-White and the Seven Dwarfs.* Illus. by Nancy Ekholm Burkert; adapted from the Brothers Grimm. [CH 1973]

Lesser, Rika. *Hansel and Gretel.* Illus. by Paul O. Zelinsky. [CH 1985]

Zelinsky, Paul O. *Rapunzel.* [CA 1998]

Wolves—Fiction

George, Jean Craighead. *Julie of the Wolves.* [NA 1973]

Wolves—Folklore

Young, Ed. *Lon Po Po: A Red-Riding Hood Story from China.* [CA 1990]

Women—France—History—18th century

Eaton, Jeanette. *A Daughter of the Seine: The Life of Madame Roland.* [NH 1930]

Woods Hole (Mass.)—Fiction

Allee, Marjorie Hill. *Jane's Island.* [NH 1932]

World history

Foster, Genevieve. *Birthdays of Freedom. Vol. 1. America's Heritage from the Ancient World.* [NH 1953]

Van Loon, Hendrik Willem. *The Story of Mankind.* [NA 1922]

World War, 1914–1918—Fiction

Mukerji, Dhan Gopal. *Gay Neck, the Story of a Pigeon.* [NA 1928]

World War, 1914–1918—Hungary—Fiction

Seredy, Kate. *The Singing Tree.* [NH 1940]

World War, 1939–1945—China—Fiction

DeJong, Meindert. *The House of Sixty Fathers.* [NH 1957]

World War, 1939–1945—Denmark—Fiction

Lowry, Lois. *Number the Stars.* [NA 1990]

World War, 1939–1945—France—Paris—Fiction

Bishop, Claire Huchet. *Pancakes-Paris.* [NH 1948]

World War, 1939–1945—Hungary—Fiction

Sawyer, Ruth. *The Christmas Anna Angel.* Illus. by Kate Seredy. [CH 1945]

World War, 1939–1945—Jews—Rescue—Fiction

Lowry, Lois. *Number the Stars.* [NA 1990]

World War, 1939–1945—Netherlands

Reiss, Johanna. *The Upstairs Room.* [NH 1973]

World War, 1939–1945—Personal narratives

Reiss, Johanna. *The Upstairs Room.* [NH 1973]

World War, 1939–1945—United States

Johnson, Gerald W. *America Moves Forward: A History for Peter.* [NH 1961]

World War, 1939–1945—United States—Fiction

Giff, Patricia Reilly. *Lily's Crossing.* [NH 1998]

Means, Florence Crannell. *The Moved-Outers.* [NH 1946]

World's Columbian Exposition (1893: Chicago, Ill.)—Fiction

Lawson, Robert. *The Great Wheel.* [NH 1958]

Worms—Fiction

Lionni, Leo. *Inch by Inch.* [CH 1961]

Wright, Orville, 1871–1948

Freedman, Russell. *The Wright Brothers: How They Invented the Airplane.* [NH 1992]

Wright, Wilbur, 1867–1912

Freedman, Russell. *The Wright Brothers: How They Invented the Airplane.* [NH 1992]

Wyoming—History—Fiction

Schmidt, Sarah. *New Land, a Novel for Boys and Girls.* [NH 1934]

Z

Zimbabwe—Fiction

Farmer, Nancy. *The Ear, the Eye, and the Arm.* [NH 1995]

Farmer, Nancy. *A Girl Named Disaster.* [NH 1997]

Zodiac—Fiction

Maxwell, William. *The Heavenly Tenants.* [NH 1947]

Zoologists—Norway—Biography

Hall, Anna Gertrude. *Nansen.* [NH 1941]

Zoos—Poetry

Seuss, Dr., pseud. (Theodor Seuss Geisel). *If I Ran the Zoo.*
[CH 1951]

Author/Illustrator Index

A

Aardema, Verna **2, 5, 33, 52, 59**
Ackerman, Karen **16, 21, 25, 40, 87**
Adams, Adrienne **18, 59, 61, 76, 78, 82**
Alexander, Lloyd **29, 53, 55**
Alger, Leclaire **32, 35, 37, 75, 81**
Allee, Marjorie Hill **56, 61, 62, 82, 90**
Andersen, H.C. (Hans Christian) **26, 47, 54, 55, 72, 79, 82, 84**
Angelo, Valenti **20, 28**
Armer, Laura Adams **5, 49, 62, 72, 79**
Armstrong, William H. **3, 20, 23, 28, 42, 69, 70**
Arthur, Malcolm **15, 26, 33, 36**
Artzybasheff, Boris **12, 20, 34, 73**
Atwater, Richard **46, 66**
Avi **36, 40, 43, 47, 57, 60, 65, 66, 74, 75, 76, 80**
Azarian, Mary **9, 10, 57, 62, 67, 75, 79**

B

Babbitt, Natalie **1, 58**
Bahti, Tom **49, 69**
Bailey, Carolyn Sherwin **20, 23, 29, 62**
Baity, Elizabeth **4, 49, 50**
Baker, Olaf **11, 49**
Bang, Molly **5, 9, 19, 30, 54, 55, 81, 83**
Bare, Arnold E. **14, 20, 39, 77**
Barnes, Nancy **19, 27, 36, 60**
Barnum, Jay Hyde **12, 73, 77**
Bartone, Elisa **12, 31, 51, 54, 63**
Baskin, Hosea **4, 6**
Baskin, Leonard **4, 6**
Baskin, Lisa **4, 6**
Baskin, Tobias **4, 6**
Bauer, Joan **7, 14, 22, 69**
Bauer, Marion Dane **1, 9, 36, 41, 45, 64**
Baylor, Byrd **22, 24, 32, 42, 49, 62, 82, 84**
Belting, Natalia M. **61, 82, 87**
Bemelmans, Ludwig **12, 13, 23, 45, 55, 66, 77, 81**
Bennett, John **46, 77**
Berry, Erick **21, 29, 30, 53**
Best, Herbert **1, 2, 31, 63**
Besterman, Catherine **29, 84, 85, 88**
Bianco, Margery Williams **12, 19, 30, 89**
Bileck, Marvin **63**
Bing, Christopher **8, 14, 68**
Birnbaum, A. **6, 14, 76**
Bishop, Claire Huchet **20, 36, 54, 60, 65, 76, 91**
Blos, Joan W. **21, 22, 30, 38, 43, 62, 80**
Blumberg, Rhoda **51, 67, 86, 87**
Bond, Nancy **28, 29, 55, 83, 84, 88**
Bontemps, Arna **3, 11, 78**
Bowen, William **1, 55, 84**
Bowman, James Cloyd **20, 46, 66**
Brink, Carol Ryrie **12, 38, 43, 90**
Brittain, Bill **55, 77, 90**
Brooks, Bruce **2, 8, 36, 57, 59, 66, 71, 80**
Brown, Marcia **2, 9, 19, 25, 26, 32, 33, 34, 36, 48, 55, 68, 74, 76, 79, 80, 84, 88, 89**
Brown, Margaret Wise **9, 11, 14, 15, 16, 47, 53, 54, 63, 76, 77, 78, 81**
Bryson, Bernarda **61, 82, 87**
Buff, Conrad **13, 19, 22, 31, 39, 41, 50, 56, 61, 83, 85**
Buff, Mary **13, 19, 22, 31, 39, 41, 50, 56, 61, 83, 85**
Bunting, Eve **14, 46, 50, 62, 71, 73**
Burglon, Nora **74, 83**
Burkert, Nancy Ekholm **24, 26, 34, 39, 81, 90**
Burton, Virginia Lee **8, 17, 25, 32, 46, 53, 73**
Byard, Carole **3, 15, 19, 27, 58**
Byars, Betsy **12, 54, 56, 82, 89**

C

Carlson, Natalie Savage **45, 66, 72, 76, 84**
Carr, Mary Jane **35, 38, 43**
Caudill, Rebecca **6, 21, 27, 30, 38, 43, 52, 74, 83, 86**
Cendrars, Blaise **2, 68, 76**
Chan, Chih-Yi **16, 33, 45, 54, 55**
Chan, Plato **16, 33, 45, 54, 55**
Charlot, Jean **5, 9, 63, 71, 78**
Chrisman, Arthur Bowie **16, 77**
Clark, Ann Nolan **5, 25, 27, 41, 45, 48, 50, 56, 60, 67, 71, 83**
Cleary, Beverly **23, 28, 30, 47, 54, 63, 65, 66, 71, 74, 79, 86**
Coatsworth, Elizabeth **7, 13, 14, 51**
Coblentz, Catherine **14, 62, 87**
Collier, Bryan **2, 8, 11, 18, 52**
Collier, Christopher **12, 19, 21, 31, 43, 87**
Collier, James Lincoln **12, 19, 21, 31, 43, 87**
Colum, Padraic **4, 7, 34, 39, 40, 42, 43, 50, 61, 75**
Coman, Carolyn **15, 28, 59, 78**
Conly, Jane Leslie **4, 21, 22, 36, 57**
Coolidge, Olivia **10, 41**
Cooney, Barbara **26, 30, 35, 62, 73, 76**
Cooper, Susan **25, 29, 55, 84, 88**
Couloumbis, Audrey **8, 21, 41, 78**
Courlander, Harold **1, 32, 77**
Crawford, Phyllis **28, 65, 73, 81**
Creech, Sharon **16, 21, 27, 36, 40, 47, 49, 64, 74, 75, 86, 88**
Crews, Donald **18, 71, 81, 85**
Cronin, Doreen **20, 85**
Curtis, Christopher Paul **3, 13, 18, 22, 27, 35, 43, 57, 70, 73**
Cushman, Karen **6, 15, 22, 25, 27, 43, 45, 58**

D

d'Aulaire, Edgar Parin **10, 54, 70**
d'Aulaire, Ingri **10, 54, 70**
Dalgliesh, Alice **9, 20, 27, 30, 37, 41, 43, 49, 53, 59, 61, 68, 83, 85**
Daugherty, James **5, 10, 12, 22, 26, 41, 46, 48, 52, 53, 54, 68, 90**
Davis, Julia **31, 43, 65, 66, 83**
Davis, Lavinia R. **3, 11, 16, 24, 35, 89**
Davis, Mary Gould **34, 47, 51**
Dayrell, Elphinstone **1, 33, 34, 59, 62, 63, 82**

de Angeli, Marguerite **4, 30, 41, 42, 43, 58, 59, 64, 67, 68, 75, 77, 85, 87**
de Paola, Tomie **8, 10, 15, 19, 21, 34, 48, 51, 57, 90**
de Regniers, Beatrice Schenk **5, 36, 53, 81**
DeJong, Meindert **15, 16, 23, 43, 67, 71, 74, 79, 81, 87, 91**
Diaz, David **14, 46, 50, 62, 71, 73**
DiCamillo, Kate **18, 23, 32**
Dillon, Diane **2, 4, 5, 25, 33, 52, 59**
Dillon, Leo **2, 4, 5, 25, 33, 52, 59**
DiTerlizzi, Tony **32, 68, 80**
Domanska, Janina **64, 68**
du Bois, William Pène **1, 5, 8, 9, 19, 29, 53, 54, 66, 88**
Duvoisin, Roger **14, 32, 56, 79, 89**

E

Eaton, Jeanette **10, 13, 18, 36, 39, 49, 63, 70, 72, 73, 80, 88, 89, 90**
Eckert, Allan W. **8, 46, 82**
Edmonds, Walter Dumaux **20, 28, 38, 43, 59, 86**
Egielski, Richard **11, 23, 46, 48, 66**
Ehlert, Lois **6, 18, 76**
Eichenberg, Fritz **4, 5, 63**
Elkin, Benjamin **22, 41, 53, 90**
Emberley, Barbara **6, 19, 32, 58, 63, 79, 81, 87**
Emberley, Ed **6, 19, 32, 58, 63, 79, 81, 87**
Engdahl, Sylvia Louise **29, 55, 72, 79**
Enright, Elizabeth **3, 13, 16, 20, 30, 48, 53, 82, 87, 90**
Estes, Eleanor **12, 19, 23, 27, 36, 48, 60, 69, 72**
Ets, Marie Hall **5, 17, 19, 26, 35, 46, 57, 68, 69, 77**

F

Falconer, Ian **9, 67**
Farmer, Nancy **1, 11, 18, 38, 46, 52, 60, 61, 75, 77, 82, 91**
Feelings, Muriel **2, 4, 19, 64, 82**
Feelings, Tom **2, 4, 19, 64, 82**
Fenner, Carol **2, 13, 39, 60**
Field, Rachel **22, 23, 29, 38, 43, 48, 56, 65, 70**
Finger, Charles **35, 49, 50, 79**

Fish, Helen Dean **47, 64, 68**
Fisher, Cyrus, pseud. (Darwin L. Teilhet) **1, 36, 80, 85**
Flack, Marjorie **12, 73, 77**
Fleischman, Paul **50, 64, 68, 77, 80**
Fleischman, Sid **1, 73, 82**
Fleming, Denise **36, 61, 69, 81**
Forbes, Esther **6, 12, 43, 47**
Ford, Lauren **7, 41, 51**
Foster, Genevieve **10, 18, 36, 39, 45, 54, 70, 86, 88, 90**
Fox, Paula **14, 42, 43, 72, 75, 78**
Frasconi, Antonio **36, 64, 68**
Freedman, Russell **1, 3, 10, 31, 54, 70, 73, 86, 91**
Freeman, Don **11, 52, 67, 74**
Fritz, Jean **16, 37**

G

Gág, Wanda **4, 14, 23, 24, 26, 33, 39, 46, 48, 55, 71, 80, 81, 90**
Gaggin, Eva Roe **36, 43, 56, 67**
Galdone, Paul **5, 15, 57, 66**
Gammell, Stephen **11, 16, 21, 25, 28, 40, 49, 87, 89**
Gannett, Ruth Chrisman **23, 34, 35, 54, 59, 74, 85**
Gannett, Ruth S. **5, 29**
Gantos, Jack **4, 7, 8, 31**
Gates, Doris **28, 58, 74**
Geisel, Theodor Seuss **6, 29, 30, 32, 48, 53, 63, 69, 81, 88, 92**
George, Jean Craighead **1, 4, 20, 25, 46, 59, 76, 82, 89, 90**
Gergely, Tibor **11, 16, 47, 81**
Giff, Patricia Reilly **7, 9, 16, 27, 35, 36, 43, 63, 65, 72, 91**
Gipson, Fred **23, 28, 38, 41, 43, 46**
Glass, Andrew **55, 64, 77, 80, 90**
Goble, Paul **45, 46, 49**
Goffstein, M. B. **3, 32, 40**
Goode, Diane **6, 28, 60, 87, 89**
Goudey, Alice E. **18, 59, 61, 76, 78, 82**
Graham, Al **19, 81, 85**
Graham, Margaret Bloy **27, 40, 72, 81**
Gray, Elizabeth Janet (Elizabeth Gray Vining) **10, 23, 41, 42, 43, 58, 64, 65, 66, 67, 71, 75, 84, 87**
Greene, Bette **2, 7, 36**
Grifalconi, Ann **1, 2, 13, 33, 56**
Grimm, Jacob **6, 24, 26, 34, 39, 60, 73, 80, 81, 90**
Grimm, Wilhelm **6, 24, 26, 34, 39, 60, 73, 80, 81, 90**

Gurko, Leo **4, 10, 26, 36, 65, 72**

H

Hader, Berta **5, 15, 22, 47, 48, 49, 79, 83, 89**
Hader, Elmer **5, 15, 22, 47, 48, 49, 79, 83, 89**
Haley, Gail E. **1, 33, 81**
Hall, Anna Gertrude **10, 26, 61, 80, 91**
Hall, Donald **30, 62, 76**
Hallock, Grace **43, 56, 77**
Hamilton, Virginia **2, 21, 28, 29, 32, 36, 39, 45, 57, 60, 61, 65, 70, 78**
Handforth, Thomas **13, 16, 22**
Havighurst, Marion **38, 43, 48, 55, 64, 65**
Havighurst, Walter **38, 43, 48, 55, 64, 65**
Hawes, Charles **21, 42, 65, 68, 74, 75, 78**
Henkes, Kevin **11, 31, 57, 66**
Henry, Marguerite **6, 13, 16, 17, 25, 45, 46, 59, 69, 89**
Herrera, Velino **50, 71, 83**
Hesse, Karen **22, 24, 30, 43, 65, 68**
Hewes, Agnes Danforth **12, 14, 18, 32, 43, 54, 62, 65, 68, 69, 72, 75**
Hiaasen, Carl **1, 13, 25, 32, 65**
Highwater, Jamake **49**
Ho, Minfong **54, 55, 78, 81, 83**
Hodges, Margaret **23, 25, 33, 34, 39, 51, 53, 64, 85**
Hogrogian, Nonny **7, 20, 32, 33, 36, 37, 73, 75**
Holbrook, Stewart **10, 79, 86, 87**
Holling, Holling C. **5, 13, 14, 41, 42, 49, 58, 73, 75, 77, 79, 85, 88**
Holm, Jennifer L. **13, 31, 38, 43, 76, 88**
Horvath, Polly **12, 35, 50, 66, 76, 85**
Howitt, Mary **32, 68, 80**
Hubbard, Ralph **12, 21, 42, 49, 60**
Hunt, Irene **8, 30, 41, 43, 47, 86**
Hunt, Mabel Leigh **6, 10, 17, 24, 27, 37, 43, 84**
Hyman, Trina Schart **23, 25, 26, 33, 34, 39, 40, 42, 53, 58, 68, 76, 83**

94 Newbery and Caldecott Awards: A Subject Index

Isadora, Rachel **48, 51, 60, 85**
Ish-Kishor, Sulamith **28, 31, 52, 83**
Issacs, Anne **38, 83**

James, M. R. **26, 54, 55, 79, 84**
James, Will **45, 46, 89**
Jarrell, Randall **9, 24, 26, 29, 34, 39, 46, 47, 54, 55, 57, 81, 90**
Jeffers, Susan **6, 64, 68**
Jewett, Eleanor **7, 40, 41, 42, 43, 58**
Johnson, Gerald W. **4, 19, 70, 86, 87, 91**
Johnson, Stephen T. **4, 6, 17**
Jones, Elizabeth Orton **9, 70**
Jones, Idwal **42, 45, 88**
Jones, Jessie Orton **9**
Joslin, Sesyle **25, 47**
Judson, Clara Ingram **10, 45, 53, 54, 70, 73, 80, 86, 87**
Jukes, Mavis **31, 80**

Kalashnikoff, Nicholas **72, 76, 77, 80**
Kalnay, Francis **7, 65, 69, 89**
Keats, Ezra Jack **2, 13, 17, 25, 79**
Keith, Harold **43, 70, 79, 80, 86, 88**
Kelly, Eric P. **31, 43, 58, 69**
Kendall, Carol **29, 48, 59, 72, 87**
Kepes, Juliet **9, 52, 58, 85**
Kerley, Barbara **7, 10, 22, 42, 58**
Kherdian, David **7, 10, 15, 52**
Kimmel, Eric **40, 42, 83**
Kingman, Lee **14, 20, 39, 77**
Konigsburg, E. L. **2, 13, 19, 37, 42, 57, 60, 63, 73, 74, 80, 83, 90**
Krauss, Ruth **5, 29, 35, 46, 48, 79, 80, 89**
Krumgold, Joseph **23, 24, 31, 37, 41, 42, 62, 76**
Kyle, Anne **6, 31, 44, 51**

Labastida, Aurora **17, 57, 69**
Langstaff, John **5, 20, 32, 81**
Langton, Jane **14, 29, 32, 46, 56**
Lasky, Kathryn **56, 61**

Latham, Jean Lee **7, 44, 61, 62, 74, 77**
Lathrop, Dorothy Pulis **6, 9, 17, 26, 29**
Lauber, Patricia **74, 88**
Lawson, Robert **5, 8, 10, 21, 22, 27, 29, 30, 31, 39, 44, 46, 47, 50, 64, 67, 68, 71, 75, 86, 91**
L'Engle, Madeleine **16, 20, 21, 22, 23, 39, 40, 50, 75, 80, 83**
Le Guin, Ursula K. **29, 55**
Leaf, Munro **8, 21, 22, 30, 75**
Lenski, Lois **19, 27, 32, 44, 49, 51, 62, 76, 82**
Lent, Blair **1, 14, 24, 33, 34, 49, 51, 59, 62, 63, 64, 82, 84, 85**
Leodhas, Sorche Nic, pseud. (Leclaire Alger) **32, 35, 37, 75, 81**
Lesser, Rika **26, 34, 39, 90**
Lester, Julius **3, 35, 52, 78, 83, 86**
Levine, Gail Carson **29**
Lewin, Betsy **20, 85**
Lewin, Ted **12, 31, 54, 63**
Lewis, Elizabeth Foreman **16, 17, 59**
Lide, Alice Alison **1, 4, 25, 77**
Lindquist, Jennie **27, 48, 83**
Lionni, Leo **6, 11, 25, 32, 56, 57, 69, 84, 89, 91**
Lipkind, William **9, 12, 15, 23, 54**
Lisle, Janet Taylor **25, 28, 37, 57**
Lobel, Anita **4, 77, 81**
Lobel, Arnold **4, 5, 26, 37, 47, 63, 77, 81, 84**
Lofting, Hugh **5, 23, 29, 46, 75**
Low, Joseph **14, 25, 27**
Lownsbery, Eloise **44, 53, 68**
Lowry, Lois **22, 27, 37, 38, 44, 52, 75, 91**

Macaulay, David **6, 14, 21, 35, 54, 66, 71**
MacDonald, Golden, pseud. (Margaret Wise Brown) **14, 53, 54, 76, 77**
MacDonald, Suse **4**
MacLachlan, Patricia **27, 37, 44, 70, 80**
Malcolmson, Anne **8, 25, 32, 53, 73**
Malkus, Alida **20, 31, 44, 56**
Marcellino, Fred **15, 26, 33, 36**
Marshall, Bernard G. **21, 35, 53**
Marshall, James **9, 26**
Martin, Ann M. **27, 37, 56, 85**

Martin, Jacqueline Briggs **9, 10, 57, 62, 67, 75, 79**
Mathis, Sharon Bell **2, 3, 8, 16, 27, 41**
Maxwell, William **19, 29, 82, 88, 90, 91**
Mazer, Norma Fox **14, 16, 21, 40**
McCarty, Peter **14, 23, 67**
McCloskey, Robert **9, 12, 18, 24, 27, 35, 39, 50, 55, 56, 59, 61, 65, 82, 83, 86, 88**
McCully, Emily Arnold **31, 66, 84**
McDermott, Beverly Brodsky **40, 52**
McDermott, Gerald **1, 5, 7, 31, 33, 34, 49, 52, 59, 62, 64, 70, 82, 85**
McGinley, Phyllis **4, 18, 23, 48, 54, 68**
McGraw, Eloise Jarvis **21, 24, 26, 27, 29, 38, 41, 44, 47, 49, 61, 76, 82, 84, 89**
McKinley, Robin **29**
McKissack, Patricia C. **2, 21, 39, 45, 77, 79, 82, 89**
McNeely, Marian Hurd **38, 44, 79**
Meade, Holly **55, 78, 81, 83**
Meader, Stephen W. **37, 44, 84**
Means, Florence Crannell **44, 51, 70, 91**
Meigs, Cornelia **4, 8, 9, 10, 13, 18, 20, 38, 44, 54, 58, 62, 65, 73, 74, 77**
Miles, Miska **3, 16, 21, 40, 50, 62**
Milhous, Katherine **24, 67**
Miller, Elizabeth **4, 44**
Minarik, Else H. **9, 16, 40**
Montgomery, Rutherford **13, 62, 71, 78**
Montresor, Beni **5, 36, 53, 81**
Moon, Grace **44, 49**
Moore, Annie Carroll **24, 29, 63**
Moore, Janet Gaylord **7**
Mordvinoff, Nicolas **9, 12, 15, 23, 54**
Mosel, Arlene **24, 34, 51**
Moss, Lloyd **19, 60, 65, 81**
Mukerji, Dhan Gopal **44, 48, 67, 90**
Murphy, Jim **15, 31, 41**
Musgrove, Margaret **2, 4, 25**
Myers, Christopher **3, 42, 68**
Myers, Walter Dean **2, 3, 28, 31, 39, 42, 68, 70**

Naylor, Phyllis Reynolds **6, 23, 89**

Author/Illustrator Index **95**

Nelson, Marilyn **2, 3, 14, 68**
Ness, Evaline **21, 25, 26, 30, 33, 35, 45, 48, 73, 74, 75, 81, 83**
Neville, Emily **14, 28, 31, 37, 63**
Newberry, Clare Turlay **6, 8, 9, 13, 14, 15, 23, 37, 71, 76**
Nicolas, pseud. (Nicolas Mordvinoff) **9, 12, 15, 23, 54**
North, Sterling **10, 15, 20, 46, 64, 71, 90**

O'Brien, Robert C. **5, 20, 29, 57, 72**
O'Dell, Scott **1, 26, 40, 41, 44, 46, 49, 50, 57, 66, 72, 76, 82**
Olds, Elizabeth **11, 31, 50**

Palazzo, Tony **19, 81, 85**
Park, Linda Sue **44, 53, 65, 69**
Parker, Robert Andrew **30, 63, 81**
Parnall, Peter **22, 24, 32, 42, 82, 84**
Parrish, Anne **4, 13, 23, 29, 47, 50, 77**
Paterson, Katherine **15, 21, 28, 31, 35, 37, 40, 41, 47, 48, 50, 54, 55, 78, 85, 88**
Paulsen, Gary **14, 23, 25, 30, 47, 58, 61, 64, 81, 82, 85, 89**
Peck, Richard **16, 20, 22, 40, 44, 48**
Peet, Bill **8, 10, 14, 48, 66, 88**
Pelletier, David **4**
Perrault, Charles **15, 26, 33, 36, 80**
Petersham, Maud **4, 47, 64, 66, 68, 86**
Petersham, Miska **4, 47, 64, 66, 68, 86**
Pilkey, Dav **46, 59, 63**
Pinkney, Andrea Davis **2, 10, 24, 51, 60, 67**
Pinkney, Brian **2, 24, 34, 35, 37, 51, 56, 60, 67, 71, 82, 89**
Pinkney, Jerry **2, 3, 10, 17, 21, 26, 35, 47, 52, 63, 72, 78, 79, 82, 83, 86, 89**
Plume, Ilse **6, 26, 34, 39, 60, 73**
Politi, Leo **5, 13, 17, 24, 42, 54, 58, 66, 69, 70, 74, 79, 82**
Pope, Elizabeth Marie **14, 24, 25, 29**
Preston, Edna Mitchell **30, 63, 81**

Priceman, Marjorie **19, 60, 65, 81**
Provensen, Alice **3, 10, 12, 36, 46**
Provensen, Martin **3, 10, 12, 36, 46**

Rankin, Louise **1, 16, 23, 48, 84, 85**
Ransome, Arthur **34, 74**
Rappaport, Doreen **2, 8, 11, 18, 52**
Raschka, Christopher **2, 19, 37, 51**
Raskin, Ellen **24, 28, 60, 61, 72, 90**
Rathmann, Peggy **1, 23, 46, 69, 74**
Rawlings, Marjorie Kinnan **29, 32, 48, 73**
Reed, Philip **59, 64, 68**
Reiss, Johanna **11, 15, 45, 52, 62, 72, 91**
Reyher, Becky **34, 35, 54, 59, 74, 85**
Rhoads, Dorothy **19, 41, 49, 56, 57, 72**
Ringgold, Faith **2, 23, 32, 42**
Robbins, Ruth **17, 35, 51, 74**
Robinson, Mabel Louise **3, 11, 50, 56, 61**
Rohmann, Eric **5, 11, 22, 37, 57, 60, 71, 81, 84**
Rojankovsky, Feodor **5, 20, 32, 81**
Rourke, Constance **7, 11, 21, 65, 68, 80, 87**
Ryan, Cheli Duran **63**
Rylant, Cynthia **6, 8, 18, 21, 28, 37, 41, 54, 55, 60, 64, 72, 87, 89**

Sachar, Louis **13, 37, 45, 52, 70**
San Souci, Robert D. **3, 17, 26, 34, 35, 37, 56, 71, 78, 79, 82, 89**
Sandoz, Mari **15, 45, 49, 72, 89**
Sauer, Julia **17, 29, 32, 48, 54, 55, 64, 88**
Sawyer, Ruth **13, 17, 19, 35, 37, 47, 62, 63, 73, 86, 91**
Say, Allen **34, 40, 45, 51, 53, 59, 86, 88**
Schaefer, Jack **13, 41, 58, 77**
Scheer, Julian **63**
Schlein, Miriam **5, 71**
Schmidt, Sarah **38, 44, 91**

Schoenherr, John **31, 61, 65, 90**
Schreiber, Georges **17, 18, 75, 76**
Scieszka, Jon **27, 47, 77**
Seeger, Elizabeth **16, 61**
Selden, George, pseud. (George Thompson) **15, 21, 29, 37, 46, 57**
Selznick, Brian **7, 10, 22, 42, 58**
Sendak, Maurice **8, 9, 16, 18, 25, 29, 40, 46, 47, 48, 58, 59, 63, 68, 71, 78**
Seredy, Kate **13, 17, 19, 20, 30, 34, 44, 47, 91**
Seuss, Dr., pseud. (Theodor Seuss Geisel) **6, 29, 30, 32, 48, 53, 63, 69, 81, 88, 92**
Sewell, Helen **67, 68, 83**
Shannon, David **9, 22**
Shannon, Monica **7, 13, 30, 59**
Shippen, Katherine B. **11, 17, 26, 53, 61, 74, 75**
Shulevitz, Uri **17, 24, 25, 33, 34, 74, 79, 84**
Sidjakov, Nicolas **17, 35, 51, 74**
Siegal, Aranka **9, 11, 16, 45, 52, 78**
Simont, Marc **5, 23, 35, 61, 80, 84, 89**
Singer, Isaac Bashevis **30, 34, 47, 52, 69, 90**
Singmaster, Elsie **44, 78, 86**
Sís, Peter **7, 11, 16, 38, 56, 67, 75, 84, 88**
Sleator, William **4, 33, 49, 84**
Slobodkin, Louis **59, 70, 78**
Small, David **11, 17, 39, 54, 70, 85**
Smith, Lane **27, 47, 77**
Snedeker, Caroline Dale **31, 37, 44, 54, 61, 71, 73, 78**
Snyder, Diane **15, 34, 51, 53, 59**
Snyder, Zilpha Keatley **13, 28, 30, 37, 55, 60, 80, 90**
Sorensen, Virginia **20, 28, 61, 66, 70**
Speare, Elizabeth George **17, 37, 38, 44, 49, 51, 54, 55, 56, 65, 71, 72, 73, 82, 90**
Sperry, Armstrong **1, 14, 18, 20, 32, 56, 69, 75, 82**
Spier, Peter **5, 10, 32, 35, 62, 63, 79, 81**
Spinelli, Jerry **7, 20, 45, 65, 67, 70, 71, 88**
St. George, Judith **11, 70**
Staples, Suzanne Fisher **13, 17, 22, 56, 64, 65**
Steele, Mary Q. **30**
Steele, William O. **44, 86**
Steig, William **12, 22, 23, 30, 35, 50, 55, 57, 67, 82**

Steptoe, John **1, 17, 27, 33, 49, 57, 78**
Stevens, Janet **3, 9, 35, 42, 71, 85, 86**
Stewart, Sarah **17, 39, 54, 85**
Stolz, Mary **20, 27, 30, 37, 57, 63, 84**
Stone, Helen **4, 18, 23, 58, 68**
Stong, Phil **31, 44, 46, 58, 59**
Swift, Hildegarde Hoyt **3, 38, 44, 54, 71, 78, 85, 86**

Taback, Simms **18, 25, 32, 33, 52, 63, 84**
Tafuri, Nancy **24, 54, 69, 81**
Taylor, Mildred D. **3, 22, 28, 44, 58, 44, 58, 69, 70**
Teilhet, Darwin L. **1, 36, 80, 85**
Thayer, Ernest Lawrence **8, 9, 14, 68**
Thompson, George **15, 21, 29, 37, 46, 57**
Thurber, James **59, 70, 78**
Tietjens, Eunice **1, 50, 56, 76, 77**
Titus, Eve **5, 15, 57, 66**
Tolan, Stephanie S. **24, 28, 64, 84**
Tomes, Margot **16, 37**
Torrey, Marjorie **47, 59, 60, 64, 67, 68, 79**
Treffinger, Carolyn **16, 20, 72**
Tresselt, Alvin **14, 32, 56, 72, 79, 89**
Trevino, Elizabeth Borton de **7, 44, 66, 80, 87**
Tudor, Tasha **19, 59, 64, 68, 81**
Tunis, Edwin **37, 68, 86, 87, 89**
Turkle, Brinton **42, 46, 56, 61, 71**
Turner, Megan Whelan **30, 55, 73**

Udry, Janice May **59, 61, 68, 84**
Ullman, James Ramsey **4, 41, 60**
Updike, John **58, 68, 76**

Van Allsburg, Chris **12, 17, 23, 30, 39, 40, 52, 55, 64, 68, 69, 71, 74**
Van Loon, Hendrik Willem **6, 90**
Van Stockum, Hilda **47, 62, 85**
Vining, Elizabeth Gray **10, 23, 41, 42, 43, 58, 64, 65, 66, 67, 71, 75, 84, 87**
Voigt, Cynthia **13, 15, 16, 23, 27, 28, 31, 40, 57, 78**

Ward, Lynd **9, 10, 46, 47, 79, 86, 87**
Weik, Mary Hays **2, 4, 42, 51, 60, 69**
Weil, Ann **1, 12, 14, 15**
Weisgard, Leonard **14, 50, 53, 54, 72, 76, 77, 89**
Weston, Christine **1, 9, 48**
Wheeler, Opal **47, 59, 64, 67, 68, 79**
White, E. B. **30, 37, 67, 80**
White, Ruth **20, 48, 88**
Whitney, Elinor **12, 42, 44, 47**
Wier, Ester **58, 65, 72, 76**
Wiese, Kurt **16, 17, 53, 89**
Wiesner, David **15, 18, 24, 25, 27, 30, 37, 67, 81**
Wilder, Laura Ingalls **12, 20, 28, 38, 44, 45, 58, 79, 83, 89, 90**
Will, pseud. (William Lipkind) **9, 12, 15, 23, 54**

Willard, Nancy **6, 11, 46, 68**
Williams, Sherley Anne **3, 15, 19, 27, 58**
Williams, Vera B. **8, 15, 27, 40, 59, 66, 74**
Wisniewski, David **21, 33, 34, 40, 51, 52, 69**
Wojciechowska, Maia **13, 20, 31, 80**
Wood, Audrey **8, 53**
Wood, Don **8, 53**
Woodward, Hildegard **3, 11, 16, 24, 35, 89**

Yashima, Taro **8, 21, 46, 51, 54, 72, 74, 83, 85**
Yates, Elizabeth **2, 3, 5, 11, 30, 35, 46, 76, 77, 78**
Yep, Laurence **3, 17, 24, 31, 45, 60, 72, 74, 78**
Yolen, Jane **16, 31, 33, 53, 61, 65, 90**
Yorinks, Arthur **11, 23, 46, 48, 66**
Young, Ed **12, 15, 16, 18, 19, 24, 26, 27, 31, 33, 34, 48, 53, 78, 90**
Young, Ella **26, 31, 34, 35, 41, 50, 75**

Zelinsky, Paul O. **26, 34, 38, 39, 83, 90**
Zemach, Harve **21, 22, 25, 33, 45, 58, 73, 81**
Zemach, Margot **6, 21, 22, 25, 33, 45, 52, 58, 73, 81**
Zion, Gene **27, 40**
Zolotow, Charlotte **18, 40, 71, 72, 81**

Title Index

A

The ABC Bunny **4, 71, 81**
Abel's Island **30, 50, 57, 82**
Abraham Lincoln **10, 54, 70**
Abraham Lincoln, Friend of the People **10, 54, 70, 86**
Abraham Lincoln's World **10, 45, 54, 70, 86**
Across Five Aprils **30, 43, 48, 86**
Adam of the Road **23, 41, 43, 58, 84**
After the Rain **14, 16, 21, 40**
Afternoon of the Elves **25, 28, 37, 57**
The Ageless Story **7, 41, 51**
Alexander and the Wind-Up Mouse **25, 57, 84**
All Alone **20, 36, 54, 60, 76**
All Around the Town **4, 18, 68**
All Falling Down **27, 40**
All in the Morning Early **35, 75, 81**
All Sail Set **14, 18, 32, 56, 75**
Along Came a Dog **15, 23**
Alphabatics **4**
Alphabet City **4, 6, 17**
Always Room for One More **32, 37, 75**
The Amazing Bone **12, 35, 55, 67**
America Is Born **4, 19, 86**
America Moves Forward **70, 87, 91**
An American ABC **4, 66, 86**
Americans Before Columbus **4, 49, 50**
America's Ethan Allen **10, 79, 86, 87**
Amos Fortune, Free Man **2, 3, 11, 35, 78**
Anansi the Spider **1, 5, 7, 33, 59, 62**
Anatole **5, 15, 57, 66**
Anatole and the Cat **5, 15, 57, 66**
... And Now Miguel **41, 42, 62, 76**
Andy and the Lion **5, 26, 46, 48, 52, 54**
The Angry Moon **4, 33, 49, 84**
The Animal Family **9, 29, 46, 47, 55, 57**
Animals of the Bible **6, 9**
Annie and the Old One **3, 16, 21, 40, 50, 62**
Anpao **49**

Ape in a Cape **4, 5, 63**
The Apple and the Arrow **31, 83**
The Apprentice of Florence **6, 31, 44, 51**
April's Kittens **6, 13, 14**
Arrow to the Sun **31, 49, 70**
Ashanti to Zulu **2, 4, 25**
Audubon **7, 11, 65**
The Avion My Uncle Flew **1, 36, 80, 85**

B

Baboushka and the Three Kings **17, 35, 51, 74**
Bambino the Clown **17, 18, 75, 76**
Banner in the Sky **4, 41, 60**
Barkis **13, 14, 23, 76**
Bartholomew and the Oobleck **29, 53, 88**
Bear Party **9, 19, 53, 66**
The Bears on Hemlock Mountain **9, 53, 59, 61**
Because of Winn Dixie **18, 23, 32**
Belle Prater's Boy **20, 48, 88**
Belling the Tiger **20, 30, 57, 84**
Ben's Trumpet **48, 51, 60, 85**
Better Known as Johnny Appleseed **6, 10, 37, 43**
Bhimsa, the Dancing Bear **1, 9, 48**
The Big Snow **5, 79, 89**
Big Tree **13, 39, 61, 85**
The Big Tree of Bunlahy **34, 50**
The Biggest Bear **9, 46, 47**
Bill Peet **8, 10, 14, 48, 66, 88**
Birthdays of Freedom **18, 36, 90**
Black and White **21, 54, 66, 71**
The Black Cauldron **29, 55**
Black Fox of Lorne **43, 75, 77, 85, 87**
The Black Pearl **1, 57, 66, 72**
The Blue Cat of Castle Town **14, 62, 87**
The Blue Sword **29**
Blue Willow **28, 58, 74**
Blueberries for Sal **9, 12, 59**
Boats on the River **12, 73, 77**
Book of Nursery and Mother Goose Rhymes **59, 64, 68**
Boy of the South Seas **1, 50, 56, 76, 77**

The Boy of the Three-Year Nap **34, 51, 53, 59**
The Boy Who Was **43, 56, 77**
Boy with a Pack **37, 44, 84**
The Bremen-Town Musicians **6, 26, 34, 39, 60, 73**
Bridge to Terabithia **21, 31, 37, 40, 41, 48, 88**
Bright Island **50, 56**
The Bronze Bow **17, 37, 44, 51, 55, 65, 72, 73**
Bud, Not Buddy **3, 22, 35, 43, 73**
By the Shores of Silver Lake **28, 38, 44, 79, 89**

C

Caddie Woodlawn **12, 38, 43, 90**
Calico Bush **22, 38, 43, 48, 56, 65**
Call It Courage **1, 20, 69, 82**
Carry On, Mr. Bowditch **7, 44, 61, 62, 74, 77**
Carver **2, 3, 14, 68**
Casey at the Bat **8, 9, 14, 68**
Castle **6, 14, 35**
The Cat Who Went to Heaven **7, 13, 14, 51**
Cathedral **6, 14**
Catherine, Called Birdy **22, 25, 27, 43, 58**
Cedric the Forester **21, 35, 53**
A Chair for My Mother **15, 27, 40, 59, 74**
Chanticleer and the Fox **26, 35, 73**
Charlotte's Web **30, 37, 67, 80**
Children of the Soil **74, 83**
A Child's Calendar **58, 68, 76**
A Child's Good Night Book **9, 63, 78**
The Christmas Anna Angel **13, 17, 19, 47, 91**
Chucaro **7, 65, 69, 89**
Cinderella, or the Little Glass Slipper **26, 33, 36, 80**
Clearing Weather **18, 44, 62, 74, 77**
Click, Clack, Moo **20, 85**
Cock-a-Doodle Doo **15, 22, 83**
The Codfish Musket **43, 54, 62, 65, 72**
Color Zoo **6, 18, 76**

Commodore Perry in the Land of the Shogun **51, 67, 86, 87**
The Contest **7, 20, 33, 73**
The Corn Grows Ripe **19, 41, 49, 56, 57, 72**
A Corner of the Universe **27, 37, 56, 85**
The Courage of Sarah Noble **20, 27, 30, 37, 43, 49**
The Cow-Tail Switch **1, 32, 77**
Crazy Lady **4, 21, 22, 36, 57**
The Cricket in Times Square **15, 21, 29, 37, 46, 57**
Crispin: The Cross of Lead **40, 43, 47, 57, 65**
Crow Boy **8, 21, 46, 51, 72, 74, 83**

Daniel Boone **10, 12, 68**
The Dark Frigate **65, 68, 74, 75**
The Dark Is Rising **25, 29, 55, 84**
The Dark Star of Itza **20, 31, 44, 56**
The Dark-Thirty **2, 39, 45, 77, 79, 82**
Dash and Dart **22, 61**
Daughter of the Mountains **1, 16, 23, 48, 84, 88**
A Daughter of the Seine **10, 36, 73, 90**
Davy Crockett **11, 21, 68, 80, 87**
A Day on Skates **47, 62, 67, 85**
The Day We Saw the Sun Come Up **59, 61, 78, 82**
Dear Mr. Henshaw **23, 54, 63, 66, 74**
The Defender **72, 76, 77, 80**
The Desert Is Theirs **22, 24, 84**
Dicey's Song **13, 15, 16, 27, 40, 57**
Dick Whittington and His Cat **15, 25, 33, 88, 89**
The Dinosaurs of Waterhouse Hawkins **7, 10, 22, 42, 58**
Dobry **7, 13, 30, 59**
Doctor De Soto **22, 35, 57**
Dogsong **23, 25, 47**
The Door in the Wall **41, 42, 43, 58**

Down Ryton Water **36, 43, 56, 67**
Downright Dencey **37, 44, 54, 61, 71**
Dragon's Gate **17, 45, 72, 78**
Dragonwings **3, 17, 24, 31, 45, 60, 74**
The Dream Coach **23, 29**
Drummer Hoff **58, 79, 81**
Duffy and the Devil **22, 25, 33, 73**
Duke Ellington **2, 10, 24, 51, 60, 67**

The Ear, the Eye, and the Arm **1, 11, 38, 52, 61, 75, 91**
The Egg Tree **24, 67**
The Egypt Game **13, 30, 37, 60**
Eleanor Roosevelt **10, 31, 70, 73**
Ella Enchanted **29**
The Emperor and the Kite **16, 31, 33, 53**
Enchantress from the Stars **29, 55, 72, 79**
Everything on a Waffle **12, 35, 50, 66, 76, 85**

Fables **5, 26**
The Fairy Circus **17, 26, 29**
The Faithful Friend **34, 35, 37, 56, 71, 82, 89**
The Family under the Bridge **45, 66, 72, 76, 84**
The Fearsome Inn **30, 69, 90**
Feather Mountain **11, 31, 50**
Figgs & Phantoms **24, 28, 72**
Finders Keepers **12, 23, 54**
A Fine White Dust **18, 37, 64, 72**
Fish for Supper **3, 32, 40**
Fish in the Air **16, 53, 89**
Five Little Monkeys **9, 52, 58, 85**
The Fledgling **14, 29, 32, 46, 56**
Floating Island **23, 50, 77**
Fly High, Fly Low **11, 52, 67, 74**
Fog Magic **29, 32, 48, 55, 64, 88**
The Fool of the World and the Flying Ship **34, 74**
The Forest Pool **5, 72, 79**
The Forgotten Daughter **31, 44, 73, 78**

Four and Twenty Blackbirds **47, 64, 68**
The Fox Went Out on a Chilly Night **32, 35, 62, 79**
Frederick **6, 57, 69, 89**
Free Fall **24, 30, 81**
Freight Train **18, 71**
Frog and Toad Are Friends **37, 47, 84**
Frog and Toad Together **37, 47, 84**
Frog Went A-Courtin' **5, 20, 32, 81**
From the Mixed-Up Files of Mrs. Basil E. Frankweiler **13, 57, 60, 61, 63, 73, 80**
Frontier Living **37, 68, 86, 87, 89**
The Funny Little Woman **24, 34, 51**

The Gammage Cup **29, 48, 59, 72, 87**
Gandhi, Fighter without a Sword **10, 18, 39, 49, 63, 80**
The Garden of Abdul Gasazi **23, 55**
The Gardener **17, 39, 54, 85**
Garram the Hunter **1, 2, 31, 63**
A Gathering of Days **21, 22, 30, 38, 43, 62, 80**
Gay Neck **44, 48, 67, 90**
George Washington **10, 39, 70, 86, 88**
George Washington's World **10, 39, 45, 70, 88**
Getting Near to Baby **8, 21, 41, 78**
Gillespie and the Guards **22, 41, 53, 90**
Ginger Pye **13, 23, 27, 60**
A Girl Named Disaster **1, 60, 77, 82, 91**
The Girl Who Loved Wild Horses **45, 46, 49**
The Giver **27, 38, 75**
The Glorious Flight **3, 10, 12, 36**
Glory of the Seas **12, 18, 32, 75**
Goggles! **2, 13, 17, 25**
The Golden Basket **13, 45, 55**
The Golden Fleece and the Heroes Who Lived before Achilles **7, 40, 51, 61**

The Golden Goblet 24, 41, 44, 61, 76
The Golden Name Day 27, 48, 83
Goldilocks and the Three Bears 9, 26
The Golem (McDermott) 40, 52
Golem (Wisniewski) 21, 33, 34, 40, 51, 52, 69
Gone-Away Lake 3, 16, 20, 48, 53, 82, 87
Good-Luck Horse 16, 33, 45, 55
The Good Master 20, 30, 47
Grandfather's Journey 40, 45, 51, 86, 88
The Graphic Alphabet 4
Graven Images 64, 77, 80
The Great Fire 15, 31, 41
The Great Gilly Hopkins 35, 55
The Great Quest 21, 42, 75, 78
The Great Wheel 31, 44, 50, 86, 91
Green Eyes 6, 14, 76
The Grey King 29, 55, 88
The Grey Lady and the Strawberry Snatcher 81

H

Hansel and Gretel 26, 34, 39, 90
The Happy Day 5, 35, 79, 80, 89
Harlem 3, 42, 68
Hatchet 14, 23, 61, 82, 89
Have You Seen My Duckling? 24, 54, 69, 81
"Have You Seen Tom Thumb?" 10, 17, 24, 84
Hawk, I'm Your Brother 32, 42
The Headless Cupid 28, 55, 80, 90
The Heavenly Tenants 19, 29, 82, 88, 90, 91
"Hello, the Boat!" 28, 65, 73, 81
Henry Fisherman 32, 88
The Hero and the Crown 29
Hershel and the Hanukkah Goblins 40, 42, 83
Hey, Al 11, 23, 46, 48, 66
The Hidden Treasure of Glaston 7, 40, 41, 42, 43, 58
Hide and Seek Fog 14, 32, 56
The High King 29, 53, 55
Hildilid's Night 63

Hitty, Her First Hundred Years 23, 29
Holes 13, 37, 45, 52, 70
Homesick 16, 37
Hondo & Fabian 14, 23, 67
Honk, the Moose 31, 44, 46, 58, 59
Hoot 1, 13, 25, 32, 65
Hope Was Here 7, 14, 22, 69
The Horsecatcher 15, 45, 49, 72, 89
Hosie's Alphabet 4, 6
The House of Sixty Fathers 16, 43, 79, 91
The House of the Scorpion 18, 38, 46, 75
The House That Jack Built 36, 64, 68
Houses from the Sea 18, 76
The Hundred Dresses 36, 48, 69, 72
The Hundred Penny Book 2, 3, 8, 16, 27, 41
Hurry Home, Candy 23, 67
Hush! A Thai Lullaby 55, 78, 81, 83

I

I, Juan de Pareja 7, 44, 66, 80, 87
If All the Seas Were One Sea 64, 68
If I Ran the Zoo 6, 29, 48, 63, 81, 92
In My Mother's House 50, 71, 83
In the Beginning 21, 32, 61
In the Forest 5, 35
In the Night Kitchen 8, 29
In the Small, Small Pond 36, 61, 69, 81
Inch by Inch 11, 56, 91
Incident at Hawk's Hill 8, 13, 46, 82
Indian Captive 44, 49, 51, 76
Invincible Louisa 4, 8, 10
Island of the Blue Dolphins 1, 46, 49, 50, 76, 82
It Could Always Be Worse 6, 52
It's Like This, Cat 14, 28, 31, 37, 63

J

Jacob Have I Loved 15, 28, 37, 40, 47, 50, 78, 85
Jambo Means Hello 2, 4, 82

Jane's Island 56, 61, 62, 82, 90
The Jazz Man 2, 4, 42, 51, 60, 69
Jennifer, Hecate, Macbeth, William McKinley, and Me, Elizabeth 2, 37, 90
Joey Pigza Loses Control 4, 7, 8, 31
John Henry 3, 35, 52, 83, 86
Johnny Tremain 6, 12, 43, 87
Joseph Had a Little Overcoat 18, 25, 33, 52, 84
Journey Cake, Ho! 35, 65, 86
Journey Outside 30
Joyful Noise 50, 68
Juanita 5, 24, 42, 54, 66, 70, 79
The Judge 21, 45, 58, 81
Julie of the Wolves 4, 20, 25, 46, 82, 90
Jumanji 12, 30, 39, 52, 68
The Jumping-Off Place 38, 44, 79
Just Me 5, 68
Justin Morgan Had a Horse 45, 59

K

Kildee House 13, 62, 71, 78
King Bidgood's in the Bathtub 8, 53
King of the Wind 6, 25, 45, 46
The King's Fifth 26, 40, 41, 44, 57
Knee Knock Rise 1, 58

L

Leader by Destiny 10, 70, 88
The Light at Tern Rock 17, 54
Like Jake and Me 31, 80
Li Lun, Lad of Courage 16, 20, 72
Lily's Crossing 9, 36, 43, 72, 91
Lincoln 10, 54, 70, 86
Lion 5, 54
Little Bear's Visit 9, 16, 40
Little Blacknose 44, 54, 71
The Little House 17, 46
The Little Island 14, 50, 76
Little Lost Lamb 53, 54, 76, 77
Little Red Riding Hood 26, 34, 39
Little Town on the Prairie 28, 38, 44, 79, 89
Lon Po Po 16, 27, 33, 78, 90
Lone Journey 10, 36, 63, 72, 89
The Loner 58, 65, 72, 76
A Long Way from Chicago 16, 20, 22, 40, 44, 48

Title Index **101**

The Long Winter 12, 28, 38, 44, 79, 89, 90

M. C. Higgins, the Great 2, 29, 60, 65, 70
Madeline 12, 55, 66, 77, 81
Madeline's Rescue 12, 23, 55, 66, 81
Magic Maize 19, 41, 50, 56
Make Way for Ducklings 12, 24, 39
Maniac Magee 7, 45, 65, 70, 71
Many Moons 59, 70, 78
The Many Ways of Seeing 7
Marshmallow 15, 37, 71
Martin's Big Words 2, 8, 11, 18, 52
The Matchlock Gun 20, 28, 38, 43, 59, 86
May I Bring a Friend? 5, 36, 53, 81
McElligot's Pool 30, 32, 48, 63, 69, 81
Meggy MacIntosh 43, 64, 65, 87
Mei Li 13, 16, 22
Men, Microscopes, and Living Things 11, 61, 74, 75
Men of Athens 10, 41
Mice Twice 14, 25, 57
The Middle Moffat 19, 27, 60
The Midwife's Apprentice 6, 15, 25, 43, 45, 58
The Mighty Hunter 47, 49
Millions of Cats 14, 46
Minn of the Mississippi 5, 58, 73, 79, 85
Miracles on Maple Hill 20, 28, 61, 66, 70
Mirandy and Brother Wind 2, 21, 89
Mirette on the High Wire 31, 66, 84
Miss Hickory 20, 23, 29, 62
Missing May 8, 21, 28, 41, 55, 89
Misty of Chincoteague 13, 16, 17, 69, 89
Moccasin Trail 21, 27, 38, 44, 47, 49, 82, 84, 89
Moja Means One 2, 19, 64, 82
The Moon Jumpers 59, 63, 68
Moorchild 26, 29, 47
"More More More," Said the Baby 8, 27, 66
The Most Wonderful Doll in the World 23, 48, 54
Mother Goose 59, 64, 68
Mother Goose and Nursery Rhymes 59, 64, 68

Mountain Born 5, 30, 46, 76, 77
Mountains Are Free 43, 65, 83
The Moved-Outers 44, 51, 70, 91
The Moves Make the Man 2, 8, 36, 57, 71
Mr. Justice Holmes 10, 45, 53, 87
Mr. Penny's Race Horse 5, 26
Mr. Popper's Penguins 46, 66
Mr. Rabbit and the Lovely Present 18, 40, 71
Mr. T. W. Anthony Woo 5, 19, 77
Mrs. Frisby and the Rats of NIMH 5, 20, 29, 57, 72
Mufaro's Beautiful Daughters 1, 17, 27, 33, 78
My Brother Sam Is Dead 12, 19, 21, 31, 43, 87
My Father's Dragon 5, 23, 29
My Friend Rabbit 5, 37, 57, 71
My Mother Is the Most Beautiful Woman in the World 34, 35, 54, 59, 74, 85
My Side of the Mountain 1, 59, 76, 82, 89

Nansen 10, 26, 61, 80, 91
New Found World 17, 26, 53
New Land 38, 44, 91
Nicholas 24, 29, 63
Nine Days to Christmas 17, 57, 69
Nino 20, 28
No, David! 9, 22
Noah's Ark (Pinkney) 10, 63
Noah's Ark (Spier) 5, 10, 63, 81
The Noonday Friends 27, 37, 63
Nothing At All 23, 48, 55
Nothing but the Truth 36, 66, 74, 80
Number the Stars 22, 27, 37, 44, 52, 91

Officer Buckle and Gloria 1, 23, 46, 69, 74
Old Ramon 13, 41, 58, 77
The Old Tobacco Shop 1, 55, 84
Old Yeller 23, 28, 38, 41, 43, 46
Olivia 9, 67
On Market Street 4, 77, 81
On My Honor 1, 9, 36, 41, 45, 64
On the Banks of Plum Creek 28, 38, 44, 58, 89

Once a Mouse 26, 34, 48, 55
1 Is One 19, 64, 81
One-Eyed Cat 14, 42, 72
One Fine Day 7, 33, 36
One Morning in Maine 9, 27, 55, 83
One Wide River to Cross 6, 19, 32, 63, 87
Onion John 23, 24, 31, 37
Ood-le-uk the Wanderer 1, 4, 25, 77
Our Eddie 28, 31, 52, 83
Our Only May Amelia 13, 31, 38, 43, 76, 88
Out of the Dust 22, 24, 30, 43, 65, 68
Out of the Flame 44, 53, 68
Outside Over There 8, 29, 40, 78
Owen 11, 31, 57, 66
Owl Moon 31, 61, 65, 90
Ox-Cart Man 30, 62, 76

Paddle-to-the-Sea 13, 14, 41, 49, 88
The Pageant of Chinese History 16, 61
Pancakes-Paris 36, 65, 91
The Paperboy 46, 59, 63
Pecos Bill 20, 46, 66
Pedro, the Angel of Olvera Street 17, 42, 54, 69, 79
Penn 10, 66, 67, 71
Peppe the Lamplighter 12, 31, 51, 54, 63
The Perilous Gard 14, 24, 25, 29
The Perilous Road 44, 86
Phebe Fairchild 19, 27
Philip Hall Likes Me, I Reckon Maybe 2, 7, 36
Pictures of Hollis Woods 7, 16, 27, 35, 63, 65
Pierre Pidgeon 14, 20, 39, 77
The Pigtail of Ah Lee Ben Loo 46, 77
The Planet of Junior Brown 2, 36, 45, 57
Play with Me 5, 46
A Pocketful of Cricket 21, 30, 74, 83
The Polar Express 17, 40, 64, 69, 71, 74
Pop Corn & Ma Goodness 30, 63, 81
Pran of Albania 4, 44
Prayer for a Child 70
Puss in Boots (Brown) 15, 26, 33, 36

Puss in Boots (Marcellino) **15, 26, 33, 36**

Q

The Quaint and Curious Quest of Johnny Longfoot **29, 84, 85, 88**
Queer Person **12, 21, 42, 49, 60**

R

Rabbit Hill **5, 29, 46, 71**
The Railroad to Freedom **3, 38, 44, 78, 85, 86**
Rain Drop Splash **72, 89**
Rain Makes Applesauce **63**
Ramona and Her Father **30, 65, 71, 79, 86**
Ramona Quimby, Age 8 **28, 47, 65, 71, 74**
Rapunzel **26, 34, 39, 90**
Rascal **10, 15, 20, 46, 64, 71, 90**
Raven **34, 49, 64, 82, 85**
Red Sails to Capri **1, 12, 14, 15**
The Relatives Came **28, 89**
Rifles for Watie **43, 70, 79, 80, 86, 88**
A Ring of Endless Light **16, 21, 22, 23, 40, 50, 83**
The Road from Home **7, 10, 15, 52**
Roger and the Fox **35, 89**
Roll of Thunder, Hear My Cry **3, 22, 28, 44, 58, 69, 70**
Roller Skates **17, 37, 62, 63, 73**
The Rooster Crows **47, 64, 68**
Rufus M. **13, 19, 27**
Rumpelstiltskin **26, 34, 39**
Runaway Papoose **44, 49**
Runner of the Mountain Tops **3, 11, 61**

S

Saint George and the Dragon **23, 25, 33, 39, 53**
Sam, Bangs & Moonshine **45, 48**
Sarah, Plain and Tall **27, 37, 44, 70, 80**
Scorpions **2, 28, 39, 42**
Seabird **42, 75, 77, 88**
Seashore Story **51, 54**
Secret of the Andes **5, 25, 27, 41, 45, 48, 50, 56, 60, 67**
The Secret River **29, 32, 48, 73**
Sector 7 **18, 25, 81**
Seven Blind Mice **12, 18, 19, 24, 26, 34, 48**

Seven Simeons **12, 20, 34, 73**
Shabanu, Daughter of the Wind **13, 17, 22, 56, 64, 65**
Shadow **2, 68, 76**
Shadow of a Bull **13, 20, 31, 80**
Shadrach **67, 71**
Shen of the Sea **16, 77**
Shiloh **6, 23, 89**
The Sign of the Beaver **37, 38, 44, 49, 56, 82**
The Silver Pencil **41, 59, 83, 85**
Sing Down the Moon **44, 50, 62**
Sing in Praise **47, 60, 67**
Sing Mother Goose **59, 64, 68, 79**
The Singing Tree **20, 30, 44, 47, 91**
A Single Shard **44, 53, 65, 69**
Skipper John's Cook **9, 19, 32, 74**
The Slave Dancer **43, 75, 78**
Small Rain **9**
Smoky Night **14, 46, 50, 62, 71, 73**
Smoky, the Cowhorse **45, 46, 89**
Snow **17, 79**
Snow White and the Seven Dwarfs (Gág) **24, 26, 33, 39, 80, 90**
Snow-White and the Seven Dwarfs (Jarrell) **24, 26, 34, 39, 81, 90**
Snowflake Bentley **9, 10, 57, 62, 67, 75, 79**
The Snowy Day **2, 79**
So You Want to Be President? **11, 70**
A Solitary Blue **23, 28, 31, 78**
Somewhere in the Darkness **31, 70**
Song and Dance Man **16, 21, 25, 40, 87**
Song of Robin Hood **8, 25, 32, 53, 73**
Song of the Pines **38, 43, 48, 55, 64, 65**
Song of the Swallows **13, 58, 74, 79, 82**
Sounder **3, 20, 23, 28, 42, 69, 70**
Spice and the Devil's Cave **14, 43, 68, 69**
The Spider and the Fly **32, 68, 80**
Starry Messenger **7, 11, 38, 56, 67, 75**
The Steadfast Tin Soldier **26, 55, 79, 84**
The Stinky Cheese Man and Other Fairly Stupid Tales **27, 47, 77**

Stone Soup **33, 36, 76, 79**
The Storm Book **72, 81**
A Story A Story **1, 33, 81**
The Story of Appleby Capple **4, 13, 47**
The Story of Jumping Mouse **49, 57**
The Story of Mankind **6, 90**
Story of the Negro **3, 11, 78**
Strawberry Girl **27, 32, 62, 82**
The Stray Dog **23**
Strega Nona **19, 34, 51, 90**
A String in the Harp **28, 29, 55, 83, 84, 88**
Sugaring Time **56, 61**
Summer of the Swans **12, 54, 56, 82, 89**
The Sun Is a Golden Earring **61, 82, 87**
Surviving the Applewhites **24, 28, 64, 84**
Swamp Angel **38, 83**
Sweet Whispers, Brother Rush **2, 28, 39, 57, 78**
Swift Rivers **38, 44, 54, 58, 65, 73**
Swimmy **32**
Swords of Steel **44, 78, 86**
Sylvester and the Magic Pebble **23, 55**

Tales from Silver Lands **35, 49, 50, 79**
The Talking Eggs **3, 17, 26, 35, 78, 79**
The Tangle-Coated Horse and Other Tales **15, 31, 34, 35, 50, 75**
Tar Beach **2, 23, 32, 42**
T-Bone, the Baby Sitter **8, 9, 15**
Ten, Nine, Eight **9, 19, 30, 55**
The Thanksgiving Story **43, 67, 68, 83**
Theodore Roosevelt, Fighting Patriot **10, 70, 73, 80**
There Was an Old Lady Who Swallowed a Fly **32, 63, 84**
These Happy Golden Years **20, 28, 38, 45, 79, 83, 89**
They Were Strong and Good **10, 27, 39, 67**
The Thief **30, 55, 73**
Thimble Summer **13, 30, 82, 90**
Thistle and Thyme **35, 75**
Three Jovial Huntsmen **6, 64, 68**
The Three Pigs **15, 27, 67**
Thy Friend, Obadiah **42, 46, 56, 61, 71**

Tibet **16, 84, 88**
Time Flies **11, 22, 60, 81, 84**
Time of Wonder **18, 50, 56, 61, 82, 88**
Timothy Turtle **19, 81, 85**
To Be a Slave **3, 78**
Tod of the Fens **12, 42, 44, 47**
Tom Paine, Freedom's Apostle **4, 10, 26, 36, 65, 72**
Tom Tit Tot **25, 26, 33, 73**
The Tombs of Atuan **29, 55**
Tops & Bottoms **3, 9, 35, 42, 71, 85, 86**
The Treasure **24, 25, 33, 84**
Tree of Freedom **6, 27, 38, 43, 52, 86**
A Tree Is Nice **61, 84**
The Truce of the Wolf and Other Tales of Old Italy **34, 47, 51**
Truck **81, 85**
The True Confessions of Charlotte Doyle **60, 75, 76**
The Trumpeter of Krakow **31, 43, 58, 69**
Tuesday **30, 37, 81**
The Twenty-One Balloons **1, 8, 29, 53, 88**
26 Fairmount Avenue **8, 10, 15, 21, 48, 57**
The Two Reds **9, 15**

The Ugly Duckling **26, 47, 72, 82**
Umbrella **51, 72, 85**
Up a Road Slowly **8, 27, 41**
Upon the Head of the Goat **9, 11, 16, 45, 52, 78**
The Upstairs Room **11, 15, 45, 52, 62, 72, 91**

Vaino **31, 43, 66**
A Very Special House **29, 46, 48**
The View from Saturday **19, 37, 42, 74, 83**

The Village of Round and Square Houses **1, 2, 13, 33, 56**
A Visit to William Blake's Inn **6, 11, 46, 68**
Volcano **74, 88**
The Voyagers **4, 39, 42, 43, 75**
The Voyages of Doctor Dolittle **5, 23, 29, 46, 75**

Walk Two Moons **16, 21, 27, 36, 40, 47, 49, 86, 88**
The Wanderer **27, 40, 64, 74, 75, 88**
Waterless Mountain **49, 62**
The Watsons Go to Birmingham—1963 **3, 13, 18, 27, 43, 57, 70**
The Wave **34, 51, 64, 85**
The Way to Start a Day **82**
Wee Gillis **8, 21, 22, 30, 75**
The Westing Game **60, 61, 90**
What Do You Say, Dear? **25, 47**
What Hearts **57, 59, 66, 80**
What Jamie Saw **15, 28, 59, 78**
Wheel on the Chimney **11, 16, 47, 81**
The Wheel on the School **74, 81, 87**
When Clay Sings **49, 69**
When I Was Young in the Mountains **6, 28, 60, 87, 89**
When Shlemiel Went to Warsaw and Other Stories **34, 47, 52, 69**
When Sophie Gets Angry — Really, Really Angry **5, 83**
When Will the World Be Mine? **5, 71**
Where the Buffaloes Begin **11, 49**
Where the Wild Things Are **29, 48**
The Whipping Boy **1, 73, 82**
Whistler's Van **42, 45, 88**
White Snow, Bright Snow **79, 89**
The White Stag **34, 47**
Why Mosquitoes Buzz in People's Ears **2, 5, 33, 52, 59**

Why the Sun and the Moon Live in the Sky **1, 33, 34, 59, 62, 63, 82**
The Wild Birthday Cake **3, 11, 16, 24**
The Windy Hill **9, 13, 20, 62**
The Winged Girl of Knossos **21, 29, 30, 53**
The Winter Room **30, 58, 64, 81, 85, 89**
Winterbound **12, 19, 30, 89**
The Wish Giver **55, 77, 90**
The Witch of Blackbird Pond **44, 71, 90**
The Witches of Worm **13, 15, 90**
The Wonder Smith and His Son **26, 34, 41, 50**
Wonderful Year **19, 27, 36, 60**
Working Cotton **3, 15, 19, 27, 58**
The Wright Brothers **1, 3, 10, 91**
Wringer **20, 67, 88**
A Wrinkle in Time **20, 39, 75, 80**

A Year Down Yonder **16, 20, 22, 40, 44, 48**
Yo! Yes? **2, 19, 37, 71**
Yolonda's Genius **2, 13, 39, 60**
Yonie Wondernose **4, 30, 41, 67**
You Can Write Chinese **17**
Young Fu of the Upper Yangtze **16, 17, 59**
Young Mac of Fort Vancouver **35, 38, 43**
Young Walter Scott **42, 43, 75**

Zin! Zin! Zin! A Violin **19, 60, 65, 81**
Zlateh the Goat and Other Stories **34, 47, 52, 69**

About the Authors

Denise Goetting is an assistant professor of library science and Head of Cataloging at Edith Garland Dupré Library at the University of Louisiana at Lafayette. Goetting earned a Bachelor of Arts in English Education/ Library Science from the University of Louisiana at Lafayette and a Master of Library Science from Louisiana State University in Baton Rouge. She has taught library science classes in children's literature, cataloging, reference, and administration at the University of Louisiana at Lafayette. She is an indexer for the *Bayou State Periodical Index: An Index to Louisiana Popular Periodicals.* She has held positions as a school librarian, head of the reference department at the Lafayette Public Library, and director of an instructional materials center at the University of Louisiana at Lafayette.

Susan Marshall Richard is an assistant professor of library science and Head of Reference at Edith Garland Dupré Library at the University of Louisiana at Lafayette. Richard has a Master of Library Science from the School of Library and Information Science and a Bachelor of Science in Elementary Education from Louisiana State University in Baton Rouge. She has certifications in both elementary education and school librarianship. She is the editor of *Notes & Tracings,* a publication of the Academic Section of the Louisiana Library Association and an indexer for the *Bayou State Periodical Index: An Index to Louisiana Popular Periodicals.* Previously she was a reference librarian at Louisiana State University Eunice and a reference librarian for the Rapides Parish Library system in Alexandria, Louisiana.

Sheryl Moore Curry is an assistant professor of library science and Head of Internet Access Services at Edith Garland Dupré Library at the University of Louisiana at Lafayette. Curry has a Master of Library and Information Science from the School of Library and Information Science at Louisiana State University in Baton Rouge, Louisiana, and a Bachelor of Arts in English from Rhodes College in Memphis, Tennessee. She is editor of the "*Review*" column for *Louisiana Libraries,* a quarterly publication of the Louisiana Library Association and an indexer for the *Bayou State Periodical Index: An Index to Louisiana Popular Periodicals.* Previously she served in various positions including general reference, serials, and children's librarian in the Houston Public Library System.

Betsy Bryan Miguez is an assistant professor of library science and general reference librarian at Edith Garland Dupré Library at the University of Louisiana at Lafayette. Miguez earned a Bachelor of Arts degree in English from Limestone College in Gaffney, South Carolina, and a Master of Library Service degree from the Graduate School of Library Service at Rutgers, The State University of New Jersey. She contributes to *Louisiana Libraries* and is an indexer for the *Bayou State Periodical Index: An Index to Louisiana Popular Periodicals.* She has taught children's literature courses at three colleges including the University of Louisiana at Lafayette and has worked in public, school, and academic libraries in New Jersey, South Carolina, and Louisiana.

www.ingramcontent.com/pod-product-compliance
Lightning Source LLC
Chambersburg PA
CBHW052051300426
44117CB00012B/2080